5x 11/15
5/16

FEB 0 1 2006

D1505698

TURKEY
in Pictures

Francesca Di Piazza

Lerner Publications Company

Contents

Lerner Publications Company
A division of Lerner Publishing Group
241 First Avenue North
Minneapolis, MN 55401 U.S.A.

Website address: www.lernerbooks.com

web enhanced @ www.vgsbooks.com

CULTURAL LIFE   46

► The Arts. Architecture. Literature. Music. Religion.
  Holidays and Festivals. Food. Sports and
  Recreation.

THE ECONOMY   58

► Agriculture. Mining and Fishing. Manufacturing
  and Industry. Service Sector. Unemployment.
  Energy and Transportation. The Future.

FOR MORE INFORMATION

Library of Congress Cataloging-in-Publication Data

DiPiazza, Francesca, 1961–
       Turkey in pictures / by Francesca DiPiazza.
          p. cm. — (Visual geography series)—rev. and expanded.
       Includes bibliographical references and index.
       ISBN 0-8225-1169-X (lib. bdg. : alk. paper)
       Turkey—Pictorial works. I. Title. II. Series: Visual geography series (Minneapolis, Minn.)
    DR417.2.D57 2005
    956.1—dc22
                                                          2004002619

Manufactured in the United States of America
1 2 3 4 5 6 – JR – 10 09 08 07 06 05

INTRODUCTION

The Republic of Turkey was born in 1923 and is a fairly new nation, still forging its identity out of a rich and complicated past. Archaeologists record what is among the first human settlements in the world there, on Turkey's Anatolian Plain at Catalhoyuk, dating from 6500 B.C. Great empires and individuals rose and fell on Turkish land over the next 8,500 years. Hittites built a walled capital city in the center of Anatolia, guarded by massive stone lions at the gates. Greek incursions along the Aegean coast of Turkey in about 1200 B.C. provided material for one of the world's greatest poets, Homer, to sing of the war on the plain of Troy. Alexander the Great conquered Anatolia, followed by the Persians. The Roman Empire gathered up Turkey in its powerful sweep. Under stable Roman administration, the most important Christian missionary, Saint Paul, was born in Tarsus in eastern Anatolia. About three hundred years later (A.D. 326), the Christian Roman emperor, Constantine, built his new capital—Constantinople—in present-day western Turkey. Then the Roman

Empire split. The eastern Roman Empire, which included Turkey, evolved into what historians call the Byzantine Empire—the heart of the Greek-speaking Christian world.

Turkish nomadic tribes began to ride out of central Asia into this world, beginning in the 600s. Five hundred years later, the Seljuk Turks brought down the Byzantine Empire and established Islam as the faith of the land. The Seljuks gave way to the Ottoman Turks, who built an empire that would last six hundred years. Constantinople, however, remained in Byzantine hands and was not taken by the Ottomans until 1453. Renamed Istanbul, it became the premier city of a vast Islamic civilization. With the onset of World War I (1914–1918), the Ottoman Empire's great culture and glory crumbled into decay. Mustafa Kemal Ataturk, the Father of the Turks, rescued Turkey from division among European powers after World War I. He pulled the Turkish people together, as the Islamic heroes of earlier centuries had done. He insisted they help him create a modern, Western-style nation

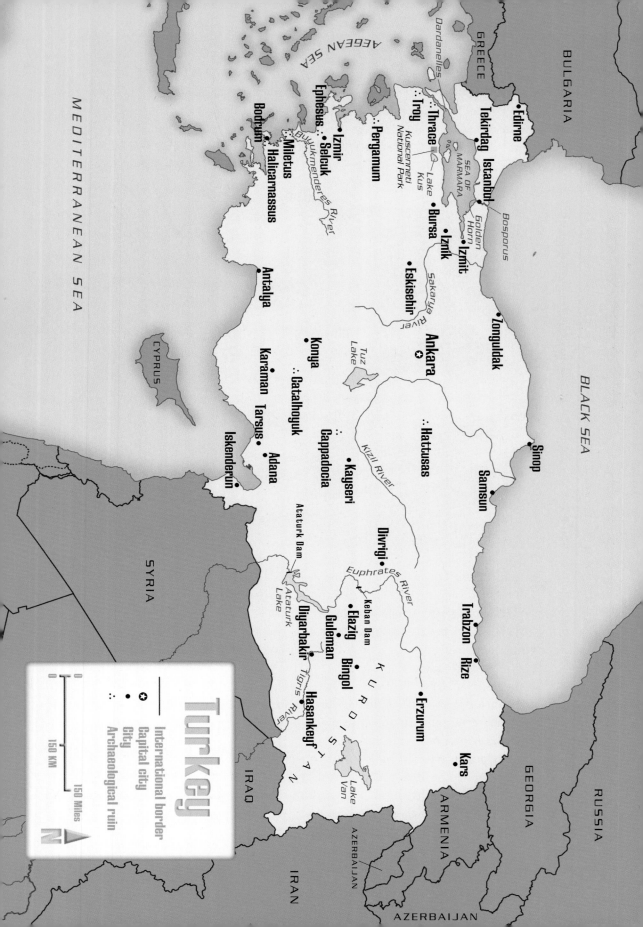

out of the ragtag remains of their once proud empire. His vision continues to shape twenty-first century Turkey.

Turkey has many gaps to bridge. Its citizens are almost entirely Muslim, and it has a strong democratic, secular (nonreligious) government. The rise of political Islam, however, challenges the ongoing development of this government. Turkey not only faces political and religious tensions within its own borders but among its Middle Eastern neighbors. Iraq, which shares Turkey's southern border, was the site of the U.S.-led war in 2003, which removed the government of dictator Saddam Hussein. The Turkish people overwhelmingly disapproved of this war, and the government offered only limited support to the United States. After the war, Turkey offered to send peacekeeping troops, but Iraqi objections forced the United States to decline the aid.

One of the biggest bridges to build is the one that will lead to Turkey's full membership in the European Union (EU), which the majority of Turks desire. The EU is an economic entity that arose in 1992 out of efforts to unite Europe politically and economically after World War II (1939–1945). The original bloc of twelve European countries continues to grow. The EU provides for trading privileges among members, with no tariffs (taxes) or limitations on movement of goods or people. Member nations may choose to use a common currency, the euro, which makes trade more stable. The EU's overall aim is to promote peace by reducing economic and social tensions that have historically led to wars. The EU requires that Turkey guarantee human rights, settle its longstanding dispute with the island nation of Cyprus, and demonstrate full democratic government.

Within Turkey, protection of the rights of individuals and of minorities, especially of the large Kurdish population in southeastern Turkey, remains weak. Historical enmity between Turkey and neighboring Greece was demonstrated in the inability to reunify the island of Cyprus, which has been divided between the two nations since the 1970s.

A new Turkish government, elected in 2002 with much popular support, offers hope that these challenges will be met. The Justice and Development Party (AKP, its Turkish acronym) has a reputation for honesty. Its leader, Prime Minister Recep Tayyip Erdogan, is a strong Muslim who is devoted to secular government and human rights. This complex and ancient land has bounteous natural resources and a large and vigorous population. If Turkey can call on all its strengths, it could indeed build a bridge to a peaceful and prosperous future.

THE LAND

Turkey straddles the boundary between the continents of Europe and Asia, but almost all of the country lies in Asia. Turkey's Asian landmass is known as Anatolia, or Asia Minor. It is composed of a large, semiarid plateau, surrounded by mountains and steep slopes. To Turkey's north lies the Black Sea. Turkey's Asian lands stretch eastward from the Straits—three bodies of water in northwestern Turkey known as the Bosporus, the Sea of Marmara, and the Dardanelles—to its eastern borders with Iran, Azerbaijan, Armenia, and Georgia. Turkey shares its southern boundary with Syria, Iraq, and the Mediterranean Sea. To the west of the Straits lies European Turkey, or Thrace, which borders Greece, Bulgaria, and the Aegean Sea. The heart of Istanbul—Turkey's largest city—lies along the European side of the Bosporus. Its large suburbs lie on the Asian side, making Istanbul the only city to span two continents. Thrace accounts for only 3 percent of Turkey's total land area, but is home to more than 10 percent of the country's population.

Topography

Because of its large size and a history of earthquakes and volcanic activity that shaped the land, Turkey has a great variety of landscapes. The country stretches over more than 300,000 square miles (777,000 square kilometers) of territory, an area that is about the size of the states of Texas and Virginia combined. Turkey has seven landform regions. Ringing the country are the Aegean, the Black Sea, and the Mediterranean regions. The interior of the country consists of the Central Plateau, the Eastern Highlands, the Pontic and Taurus mountains, and the Arabian Platform.

The densely populated Aegean Region, which includes all of Thrace, encircles the Sea of Marmara. The rolling landscape of Thrace is on the north side of the sea. Thrace is bordered on the northeast by the Istranca Mountains and on the southwest by the heights of the Gallipoli Peninsula. Despite its small size in relation to the rest of the nation, Thrace has occupied an important position in Turkish politics and economics. Istanbul, located mostly in Thrace, controls the Straits, one of the world's most important waterways. The region is home to most of the Turkish population. In addition, fertile valleys and hillsides make Thrace a valuable part of Turkey's agricultural resources.

About half of Turkey's richest farmland is in the Asian side of the Aegean Region, in broad valleys such as the Plains of Troy. These fertile lowlands receive plenty of rain. The sunny, warm climate allows farmers to cultivate olives, figs, grapes, and citrus fruits. The country's third largest city and a major manufacturing center, Izmir, is located here.

The steep coast of northern Anatolia forms the Black Sea Region. Forested mountains separate the coast from the interior. The coast widens along the Black Sea between the towns of Zonguldak and Rize into a delta area that is well watered and has a mild climate. Commercial farming thrives in the fertile strip between coast and sea. Miles of cherry groves are found here, and tea plants grow on the hillsides. Coal mining and heavy industry are centered in the western part of the region.

In the Mediterranean Region, or Turkish Riviera, the plains along the shores of the Mediterranean Sea in southern Anatolia have good soil and a warm climate particularly suited to growing citrus fruits, grapes, and various vegetables and grains. Rice and cotton are also cultivated here, in irrigated areas. Cotton textiles are manufactured in the region's Cukur Ova Plain. Pleasant weather and sandy beaches also make these coastal plains a popular tourist destination.

In a field in southern Turkey, a Kurdish girl is **picking cotton.** Turkey produces more than three million bales of cotton annually.

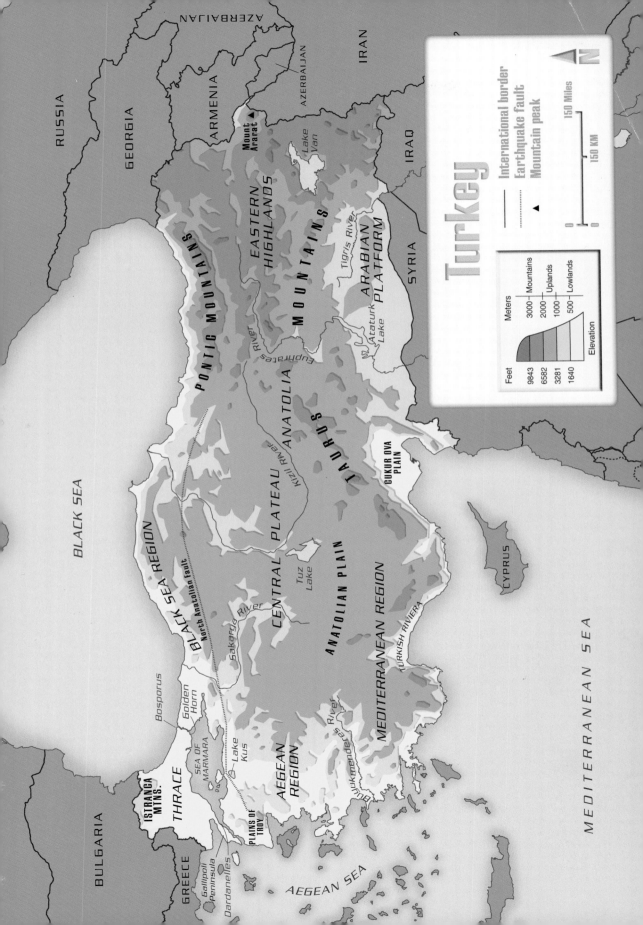

Turkey

International border
Earthquake fault
▲ Mountain peak

Feet	Meters		
9843	3000	— Mountains	
6582	2000	— Uplands	
3281	1000		
1640	500	— Lowlands	
		Elevation	

0   150 Miles
0   150 KM

N

RUSSIA

GEORGIA

AZERBAIJAN

ARMENIA

AZERBAIJAN

IRAN

Mount Ararat ▲

Lake Van

IRAQ

SYRIA

EASTERN HIGHLANDS

PONTIC MOUNTAINS

MOUNTAINS

Tigris River

ARABIAN PLATFORM

Euphrates River

ANATOLIA

Ataturk Lake

BLACK SEA

BLACK SEA REGION

North Anatolian fault

CENTRAL PLATEAU

TAURUS

ÇUKUR OVA PLAIN

Kızıl River

Sakarya River

Tuz Lake

ANATOLIAN PLAIN

MEDITERRANEAN REGION

Bosporus

Golden Horn

SEA OF MARMARA

Lake Kus

River

Sal River

TURKISH RIVIERA

BULGARIA

GREECE

ISTRANCA MTNS.

THRACE

Gallipoli Peninsula

Dardanelles

PLAINS OF TROY

AEGEAN REGION

Büyükmenderes River

AEGEAN SEA

CYPRUS

MEDITERRANEAN SEA

The heartland of Anatolia is known as the Central Plateau. Covering about 80 percent of the land surface, the plateau is characterized by rough, hilly terrain unsuited to large-scale agriculture but good for grazing goats and sheep. Overgrazing has led to soil erosion, and dust storms are frequent during the hot, dry summers. Many of the region's rivers dry up in the heat, but irrigation has allowed the cultivation of barley, pistachios and other nuts, fruits, and roses. Wheat is the principal crop. The region has several large saltwater lakes, including Tuz Lake, which lies nearly 3,000 feet (915 meters) above sea level in west-central Turkey.

Read more about Turkey's landforms, flora and fauna, and environmental challenges by going to www.vgsbooks.com for links.

In eastern Anatolia, the Eastern Highlands region has barren plains and rugged mountains, including Mount Ararat, or Agri Dagi in Turkish. At 16,949 feet (5,166 m), it is Turkey's highest peak. These highlands rise above lava-covered plateaus that are occasionally interrupted by basins, the exposed cones of once-active volcanoes—proof of recent geological activity in the region. Sometimes the basins contain lakes, such as Lake Van—a huge, slightly salty body of water that is about the size of the state of Rhode Island. Winters in the region are long and severe, with heavy snowfalls and temperatures as low as –43°F (–43°C). Summers are hot and dry. A few valleys and plains support small farms.

The Pontic and Taurus mountain ranges separate the Anatolian interior from the northern and southern coasts. Spiking to over 10,000 feet (3,048 m), they limit inland access and have isolated the coasts throughout history. To the north, the Pontic Mountains (Dogukaradeniz Daglari in Turkish, also called the North Anatolian Mountains) follow the southern shores of the Black Sea. Northwest-facing slopes tend to be heavily forested with both deciduous (leaf-shedding) and evergreen trees. The Taurus Mountains in the south extend along the Mediterranean coast and eastward to the Syrian border. Formed from limestone, these mountains have many caves and underground streams.

The Arabian Platform region is in southeastern Anatolia. High mountains to the north give way to rolling hills and a broad plateau that produces wheat and barley. This is the driest part of the country. Summers are extremely hot, with temperatures up to 115°F (46°C). Irrigation projects are increasing the variety of crops that can be grown here.

Seas, Rivers, and Lakes

Turkey has access to important regional and international seas. To the north is the Black Sea, which resembles an inland lake because it is surrounded by six countries: Turkey, Bulgaria, Romania, Ukraine, Russia, and Georgia. Water routes to the Black Sea exist only from the Aegean and Mediterranean seas located to the south. During the Ottoman period, Turkey's control of the eastern Mediterranean and Aegean seas shaped trading patterns with Europe for five centuries.

The Straits join the Aegean Sea off Turkey's west coast to the Black Sea and, until the invention of the airplane, were among the most strategic trade connections in the world. The northern part of the Straits is the Bosporus, a narrow (16-mi. or 26-km-long) channel that cuts through the city of Istanbul and ranges in width from 2 miles (3 km) to 0.3 miles (0.5 km), with a depth of up to 400 feet (122 m).

The Bosporus is connected to the Dardanelles via the Sea of Marmara, an inland body of water that is 125 miles (201 km) long and 60 miles (97 km) wide. The Dardanelles, sometimes called by its ancient Greek name, Hellespont, is 25 miles (40 km) long, ranges from 2.5 to 4.5 miles (4 to 7 km) in width, and empties into the Aegean Sea.

Two of the most important rivers in the Middle East begin in Turkey. The Euphrates River (called the Firat in Turkish) has its headwaters near Elazig and flows southward into Syria and then eastward

Ships make their way through the Dardanelles.

Young people play along the **Tigris River** in Hasankeyf. The Ilisu Dam, a part of the Southeast Anatolia Project, is designed to flood the area.

into Iraq. The Tigris River (the Dicle in Turkish) has its source close to the Euphrates and flows south past the important oil-producing area of Mosul in Iraq and the Iraqi capital of Baghdad.

The Tigris and Euphrates rivers form the Fertile Crescent, a delta region with rich soil and plenty of water, where some of the earliest civilizations in the Middle East began. In Turkey, however, these rivers pass through steep mountain gorges. The Southeast Anatolia Project (GAP, its Turkish acronym) is constructing a series of dams on the Tigris and Euphrates slated for completion in 2005. The dams bring irrigation for arid lands, employment for workers, and hydro-electric power for homes and industry. Turkey's control of this water, a vital resource in the Middle East, is a point of tension with its down-stream neighbors, Syria and Iraq.

Three other major rivers irrigate Turkey too. The Buyukmenderes River empties into the Aegean Sea. The Sakarya and Kizil rivers drain into the the Black Sea.

The varied geology of Turkey has given rise to many lakes. In mountainous regions, lakes form within limestone basins, called *ova* in Turkish. Tuz Lake in the Central Plateau (Anatolian Plain) is a basin lake. Turkey's largest lake, Lake Van in southeastern Turkey, was formed when a volcano's lava dammed its natural outflow. Some lakes are stopover places for migrating birds. Every year two to three million birds of 255 species visit Kuscenneti (Bird Paradise) National Park on the shores of Lake Kus (Bird Lake), south of the Sea of Marmara. GAP dams create new lakes, such as Ataturk Lake, which filled up behind the massive Ataturk Dam on the Euphrates when it was built in 1992.

Climate

Turkey's topography greatly influences its climate. Its seasonal variations in temperature are among the widest on earth. The areas along the coasts of Anatolia—in the narrow, lowland strips at the foot of the mountains—are characterized by cool winters and hot summers, averaging 42°F to 90°F (6°C to 32°C). The southern Anatolian coast has a very warm climate and is known as the Turkish Riviera. It is a region of palm trees and of mild seas that are ideal for swimming.

Inland, the climate changes greatly. Rainfall, which averages 20 to 30 inches (50 to 76 centimeters) annually along the coast, is greater in the mountains. It then tapers off in the dry grasslands of the Central Plateau. The city of Karaman, for example, receives only 14 inches (35 cm) of rain annually. Inland summer temperatures average about 70°F

One of the driest spots in Turkey is the the Kizil Vadi, or Red Valley, in the Cappadocia region of the Central Plateau.

(21°C). Winter temperatures in the central region hover around the freezing point.

Winters in the east are very dry, except in the mountainous regions, which are blanketed by heavy snows and are characterized by bitterly cold temperatures. Kars, for example, a city near the Armenian border, has recorded temperatures of –40°F (–40°C).

Flora and Fauna

The western and southern coasts of Turkey feature Mediterranean plant life, with groves of pine, oak, chestnut, juniper, olive, and citrus trees. The coast of the Black Sea supports laurel and myrtle plants, as well as strawberry trees (European evergreens). The mountain areas along the Black Sea have more densely forested land, where stands of oak, elm, and beech trees are found. The Central Plateau of Anatolia is a semiarid zone of grassy pastures and scattered forests. Few trees grow in the area, but low-level vegetation, such as vetches, spurges, and bulbs, are among the many plants that thrive there.

Since Anatolia has been very heavily populated for more than three thousand years, the numbers of wild animals and their habitats have decreased with the advance of human settlement. The Anatolian leopard, which lives only in Turkey, is close to extinction. Nevertheless, deer, bears, wolves, and wild boars still live in the region. Because a bird migration route between the Middle East and northern Europe crosses Turkey, a rich diversity of bird life from vultures to flamingos exists in the country. Bird preserves have been established in several places.

WILD ORCHID ICE CREAM

Environmentalists are calling for a ban on salep ice cream. Salep is flour made from a wild orchid that grows only in Turkey. Turks have been eating orchids since Ottoman times, when they were considered an aphrodisiac (something that arouses desire). The ice cream is so popular among Turks in the twenty-first century, however, that the orchid has become endangered. One ice cream manufacturer in Turkey uses twelve million flowers every year.

Turkey's coasts are rich with sea life. Fishers catch mackerel, anchovies, shrimp, and more. Some sea life is threatened by loss of habitat, pollution, and overfishing. The coastal breeding grounds of endangered monk seals and loggerhead turtles are specially protected by the government.

Cities

Turkey has had four capitals since the fourteenth century A.D. The first Ottoman capital was Bursa, located in northwestern Anatolia. (Twenty-first-century Bursa has a population of one million people and is Turkey's fifth

One blue eye and one amber (yellow) eye is another characteristic of Van cats.

Tourists survey the Istanbul skyline from a cruise ship on the Bosporus. The Blue Mosque (Islamic house of worship) appears on the left and the Hagia Sophia basilica (large church) on the right.

largest city.) Ottoman conquests into Europe led to the selection of Adrianople (named after the second century A.D. Roman emperor Hadrian) as the second capital in the late fourteenth century. (Adrianople is present-day Edirne, population 115,000.) Ottoman Turks captured Constantinople in 1453 and made it their third capital, renaming it Istanbul. After the end of World War I, Mustafa Kemal Ataturk—the founder of modern Turkey—moved the Turkish capital to Ankara, located in central Anatolia. Ataturk wanted the capital to be in the heart of the country.

ISTANBUL (population 8.9 million) is the largest and most developed city in the country and, while no longer the capital of the country, it remains its preeminent city. Linking Europe and Asia, it is a center for tourism, trade, and transportation. Turkey's main port is there, and ships are built and repaired along the Bosporus. Factory production makes Istanbul the manufacturing center of the country. Rapid growth from the immigration of thousands of villagers looking for work has strained Istanbul's resources. Affordable, safe housing is scarce, and air and water pollution are serious concerns.

Istanbul is separated by water at two places, dividing the city into three parts linked by bridges. The eastern section of Istanbul, on the Asiatic side of the Bosporus, is mostly residential suburbs, factories, and port facilities. All trains going east into Anatolia leave from Haydarpasa, the train station there. The more populous European side of Istanbul consists of two areas separated by the Golden Horn, a 5-mile (8-km) estuary (the arm of a sea where it meets a river) of the Bosporus. Beyoglu, the northern section, is the main business section and hosts luxury hotels and foreign consulates. Traditionally, it has also been home to the city's low-income groups, who live in crowded alleyways and in more modern suburbs. The skyline of Old Istanbul, on the southern side of the Golden Horn, is dominated by the minaret spires (tall, slender towers) of the Blue Mosque (Islamic house of worship). The Roman Hippodrome (racecourse), the large Byzantine basilica Hagia Sophia (from the Greek, meaning "Divine Wisdom"), and Topkapi Palace (the seat of Ottoman sultans, or rulers) are among the many other tributes to centuries of history.

ANKARA, the Turkish capital since 1923, has a population of 3.2 million. The area around Ankara has been populated since Neolithic, or Stone Age, times (CA. 6500 B.C.). Established on the site of a thirteenth-century B.C. Hittite town, Ankara had a long history of Greek, Roman, and Byzantine rule before being taken by the Ottomans in 1356. The world-class Museum of Anatolian Civilizations in Ankara records this multilayered history. The city became the focus of the nationalists during the Turkish War of Independence (1920–1922). Ataturk set about planning a modern capital along European lines, and Ankara has many government and diplomatic buildings lining spacious boulevards. Government remains its main business.

Ankara's broad streets lend it a European air, but other details are distinctly local. This outdoor sculpture of a stag with a bull on each side of it *(near right)* is a replica of a bronze filial, or decorative tip of a ceremonial staff (CA. 2300 B.C.) from another capital city, Hattusas. In modern times, a World Heritage Site about 124 miles (200 km) east of Ankara marks Hattusas, the capital of the Hittite empire.

IZMIR, formerly called Smyrna by the Greeks, has 2.7 million inhabitants and is a major port and trading center on the Aegean Sea. The bay at Izmir is polluted, but the nearby coast has many seaside resort towns. Largely rebuilt after a disastrous fire in 1922, Izmir is at the center of a region rich in Greco-Roman history. The ruins at Pergamum (Bergama in Turkish) and Ephesus (Efes) draw archaeologists and visitors from around the world. The area also is renowned for its delicious figs and seedless grapes.

ADANA is Turkey's fourth largest city. Noisy and bustling, it is home to 1.7 million people. Located inland from the eastern Mediterranean coast in the fertile Cukur Ova Plain, Adana's prosperity comes from local industry.

Environmental Issues

Air pollution in Turkish cities is caused by coal-based heating systems and industrial and automobile emissions. The introduction of clean natural gas has eased the problem in Istanbul and other major cities. Indoor air pollution is caused by heavy cigarette smoking.

Environmentalists are concerned about Turkey's plans to build its first nuclear power station. Turkey is prone to earthquakes and is therefore at higher risk for nuclear accidents. The government suspended plans for nuclear power in 2000 for budget reasons.

Turkey also struggles with water pollution. In the Black Sea, oil tankers are of environmental concern because of the high risk of

EARTHQUAKES

In May 2003, eighty-three schoolchildren and one schoolteacher in southeastern Turkey were killed when an earthquake caused their dormitory to collapse on them. The quake measured 6.4 on the Richter scale and lasted just seventeen seconds. Four years earlier, more than twenty thousand people were killed when an earthquake hit the cities of Izmit and Istanbul in August 1999.

Turkey's landmass is a small tectonic plate, constantly squeezed between two giant tectonic plates. Tectonic plates make up the surface of the earth and are always shifting in response to slow-moving, hot rock in the earth's mantle. When the plate breaks under pressure, it fractures along a fault line, causing an earthquake. Turkey's North Anatolian Fault makes the area that includes Istanbul one of the most active earthquake zones in the world. In the past two thousand years, six hundred earthquakes have been documented in the region.

spillage or collision. Tankers travel between the Black and the Mediterranean seas through the dangerously narrow Bosporus, which cuts through Turkey's largest city, Istanbul. Plans are being considered to construct a pipeline to decrease reliance on tankers.

Natural Resources

Turkey has a wealth of natural resources. Fertile soil and a great variety of climates permit the cultivation of a wide range of crops, including grains and fruits. Cotton and tobacco are major exports. Livestock is raised on ample grazing lands. Turkey is one of the few countries in the world that is self-sufficient in food.

Water is an important resource for Turkey and its neighbors. Turkey's Southeast Anatolian Project is a system of dams and hydropower plants on the Tigris and Euphrates rivers. This system provides much-needed electricity and water for urban areas and irrigation. All villages in Turkey have electricity. Irrigation helps reduce soil erosion, caused by deforestation (the removal of trees that hold soil in place), farming dry land, and overgrazing.

The country also has minerals that provide raw materials for industry. Turkey has reserves of coal, petroleum, and natural gas. Chromium is the most valuable mineral for foreign export. With its many natural ports, Turkey has a lively shipping industry. The country's forests provide firewood, but forestry adds little to the economy, as the forests are not well managed.

HISTORY AND GOVERNMENT

Humans inhabited Turkey so long ago that no written historical records of these early peoples exist. Archaeologists, however, have investigated ancient sites in Anatolia and have found abundant evidence of prehistoric settlements. Among the most exciting finds are those of a Neolithic community at Catalhoyuk, near modern Konya. This may be the world's first urban settlement.

Hittites and Assyrians

Turkey's written history began about four thousand years ago. At that time, the Hittites, a warrior group that originated in the Caucasus Mountains of eastern Europe, lived in Anatolia. Knowledge of these peoples comes from clay-tablet writings kept by Assyrians, foreign merchants living in Anatolia who traded with the Hittites. By about 1750 B.C., the Hittites had united into a single, powerful kingdom, which began absorbing realms to the south.

Under a succession of able kings, the Hittites expanded in all directions, bringing many different peoples and cultures—including the Egyptians and Syrians—into their empire. The empire prospered until about 1200 B.C., when the Phrygians, clients of the Hittites, destroyed the Hittite capital, Hattusas. Various nations of peoples on the move, called the Sea Peoples by the Egyptians, ravaged the Aegean and Mediterranean coasts and helped bring the Hittite Empire to a close.

Around the same tumultous time in Anatolia, the city of Troy (or Ilium in Greek, Tuvas in Turkish), strategically located on the Dardanelles, was also plundered and burned. About four hundred years later, the Greek poet Homer retold the legend of the Trojan War in his classic epics the *Iliad* and the *Odyssey*. There is no historical proof of exactly what happened.

During the twelfth to ninth centuries B.C., regional political units—such as the Phrygian and Lydian kingdoms—developed in Turkey amidst turmoil. During the Aegean's Dark Age (1050–800 B.C.), the Assyrian Empire in Mesopotamia (Iraq in modern times) was an aggressive force, Greece was invaded at this time by Dorians, and the Sea Peoples continued to cause regional turmoil.

Greeks and Persians

In the eighth century B.C., Greeks—Dorians, Ionians, and Aeolians—began to cross the Aegean Sea and to settle along the western shores of present-day Turkey. Through Greek influence, cities such as Ephesus, Halicarnassus, Miletus, and Troy prospered as trading centers.

By the sixth century B.C., the Lydians had conquered most of the Greek cities and had amassed great wealth. Croesus, the last king of Lydia, extended his empire over much of Anatolia and sought to increase his wealth and power by conquest. He fought against the Persian Empire located to the east but was defeated in battle in 546 B.C.

The Greek cities of Asia Minor remained under the control of their new Persian overlords for several centuries. With the help of Greeks from Athens, the Greeks of Asia revolted against the Persians in 499 B.C. Although they made repeated attempts to defeat the Greeks, the Persians were beaten in battle after battle.

In 334 B.C., Alexander the Great, the king of Macedon—an area in northwestern Greece that included Thrace—crossed the Dardanelles to destroy the Persian Empire in Asia Minor. At the time of his death in 323 B.C., Alexander the Great ruled over the largest empire, including all of present-day Turkey, that the ancient world had ever known.

Alexander the Great sits before a ritual fire the night before a battle. A priest conducts a religious ceremony for the occasion.

The Roman and Byzantine Empires

After Alexander's death, his empire crumbled into many small factions. The resulting political and economic turmoil lasted for more than two centuries until the area, including much of modern Turkey, was added to the Roman Empire in 138 B.C. Roman rule brought security and prosperity to Asia Minor for several hundred years. Roman practices drove law and administration while culture and language remained Greek. The Christian religion came to the Roman world—including Turkey—in large part through the Greek-speaking missionary Saint Paul, in the mid-first century A.D.

The eastern part of the Roman Empire became so economically important that in A.D. 326, the Roman emperor Constantine I moved his capital from Rome to the old Greek city of Byzantium on the shores of the Bosporus. On this site, he built a modern capital called New Rome, soon renamed Constantinople (Constantine's City).

With Constantine's conversion to Christianity, Constantinople became the seat of the Christianized Roman Empire. In 395, as part of an empirewide reorganization, the Latin-speaking western section of the empire was separated from the Greek-speaking eastern part. Thereafter, Constantinople was the center of the eastern realm, later called the Byzantine Empire. The church of Hagia Sophia was built in Constantinople under the orders of the Byzantine emperor Justinian in 532. This architectural marvel became the spiritual center of the Greek Christian world.

By the seventh century, the empire included all of Anatolia and Greece, as well as Syria, Egypt, most of Italy, and parts of North Africa and the Balkans (eastern Europe). As the richest area of the empire, Anatolia provided the largest portion of the fighting force that protected the far-reaching imperial borders.

The first great threat to the Byzantine Empire came from Arab warriors who were inspired by the religion of Islam, which arose in the seventh century A.D. Islam also spread through Muslim (practitioners of Islam) merchants, who traveled in caravans through the Middle East to sell spices and other luxuries. Although slowly diminishing in size, the Byzantine Empire also survived attacks by Slavic, Persian, and Germanic invaders.

In the eleventh century, Christian armies from Western Europe organized into religious pilgrimages called the Crusades. They passed through Constantinople on their way to Jerusalem, which the crusaders aimed to recapture from Islamic armies. In 1204, however, the members of the Fourth Crusade, supported by the

These monumental bronze and gold horses and other **Byzantine art objects** were taken from the Hippodrome in Constantinople (Istanbul) in 1204 by Venetian members of the Fourth Crusade. In modern times, they have long been a symbol of Venice, Italy, where they stand over the entrance doors of San Marco (Saint Mark's) Church.

city-state of Venice, captured and looted Constantinople, Venice's rival in trade. Two thousand residents were killed. The crusaders established a state, called the Latin Empire, and the Byzantine government did not regain control of Constantinople until 1261.

Turks and Ottoman Rule

During the tenth century, Turkish nomads (roaming pastoral people) began moving into Anatolia. These peoples from the arid steppes (grasslands) of central Asia were forced out of their homeland, called Turkistan, by the Mongols, a stronger Asian group. From contact with Arabs, the Turks adopted the Islamic religion. One group of Turks, the Seljuks, seized political control of almost all of Anatolia and established a kingdom called the Sultanate of Rum (an alternate spelling of Rome) in the twelfth century. Conversion to Islam and Turkish culture in Anatolia progressed under the Seljuks.

During the thirteenth century, in a small district of north-western Anatolia, a Turk named Ertugrul became the local ruler and founder of the dynasty (ruling family) of Ottoman Turks. In the six centuries that followed, Ertugrul's descendants expanded their rule to include most of the Middle East and large parts of Europe and North Africa. The name Ottoman is derived from Osman, the name of Ertugrul's son and successor.

The Ottoman Turks expanded their authority rapidly at the expense of the Byzantine Greeks and the collapsing Seljuks. Under Sultan Orhan I, the Ottomans crossed the Dardanelles in 1345 and gained their first foothold in Europe at Gallipoli, from where they proceeded to invade much of the Western world. The Ottoman Empire progressed with the help of Christian kings in the Balkans who invited the Ottomans to settle conflicts with other rulers.

As evidence of their success in Europe, the Turks moved their capital in 1366 from Bursa in Anatolia to Adrianople in eastern Europe. Kingdoms in Serbia, Romania, and Bulgaria fell to the Turks, but the Turks failed to capture Constantinople, the only remnant of the Byzantine Empire, for nearly one hundred years.

On May 29, 1453, after a fifty-day siege of Constantinople, the Turks stormed the city and seized the capital. The Turks renamed it Istanbul, from the Greek phrase *eis tan polin,* or "to the city." Sultan Mehmet II, who became known as Mehmet the Conqueror, immediately ordered the famous Byzantine church of Hagia Sophia to be converted into a mosque. This change signaled the transformation of Christian Constantinople into the capital and holy city of a great Islamic empire. According to a census taken twenty-five years later, 60 percent of all households in Istanbul were Muslim. Christians and Jews were allowed to follow their own religions, but with the fall of Constantinople, the Byzantine Empire had come to an end.

By the mid-fifteenth century, the Turks had taken over the lands and the cultures of great civilizations in the Middle East, Anatolia, and southeast Europe. Islam provided the Ottoman Turks with the Arabic script as well as with the essentials of the Islamic religion and culture. The sultan became both absolute leader of the empire's civil government and caliph (head of the Islamic religion).

Visit www.vgsbooks.com for links to websites with more information about Turkey's long and colorful past, from Catalhoyuk in 9,000 B.C., through six hundred years of Ottoman rule, to modern times.

The center of Ottoman power after 1453 was Topkapi (Cannon Gate) Palace in Istanbul. The sultan and his entire court lived there, in the largest palace grounds in Europe. The sultan presided over a council of advisers called the divan, as well as over a number of schools for educating young people for jobs in the imperial bureaucracy. A few individuals in government jobs attained high office—some reaching the post of grand vizier, the most powerful adviser in the divan.

Suleyman the Magnificent and the Janissaries

Suleyman I ruled the Ottoman Empire from 1520 to 1566. By the end of his long rule, he had created the most powerful empire in the world. He became known as Suleyman the Magnificent by the peoples he conquered in Europe. His armies took Budapest, Hungary, in 1521 but failed to take Vienna in 1529. He fostered trade with European states and extended his empire's borders to the west through North Africa and to the east through Mesopotamia. Called the Lawgiver by Turks,

Suleyman the Magnificent kept a diary. On August 31, 1526, he wrote, "Rain falls in torrents. Two thousand prisoners executed."

he oversaw the codification of administrative and Islamic law based on the Quran (the holy book of Islam) and was a patron of the arts and sciences. When Suleyman died in 1566, Constantinople was the most populous city in Europe, with a population of about 500,000 people.

Through conquest, the Ottomans acquired many slaves and prisoners of war. Some of them were the children of Christians from captive regions such as Greece or the Balkan provinces of southeastern Europe. One-fifth of all slaves became the sultan's property. Some women and girls became part of the sultan's harem (secluded quarters reserved for women, children, and their attendants) or servants of court women in the royal court in Istanbul. Some male slaves were converted to Islam, educated, and organized into a highly trained fighting legion called the Janissary Corps (taken from *yeniceri*, Turkish for "new troops"). The corps served both as an imperial bodyguard and as an elite unit of the Turkish army.

The corps eventually numbered more than 135,000 members, and as the Turkish state became involved in fewer wars, the restless Janissaries began to turn their energies to politics. Originally fiercely loyal only to the sultan, the corps eventually became a disruptive force that could support or depose the sultan at will. When the power of the sultans started to decline in the seventeenth century, the Janissaries removed or killed officials they did not like and shaped state policy to their own advantage.

Another powerful aspect of sultanic leadership was the ruler's harem. (Having up to four wives at a time was an accepted part of the Islamic religion.) Except within the family structure, Ottoman women in general had little power or visibility. High-ranking royal women, however, came to have great political power, especially in the sixteenth through the seventeenth centuries, which became known as the

THE CAGE

Sultans in the Ottoman Empire practiced fratricide, the execution of brothers who might threaten their reign. When Mehmet III, the great-grandson of Suleyman I, took the throne in 1595, he had his nineteen brothers killed, and all his sisters too, just in case. After 1603, however, fratricide was replaced with the institution of the Cage, or *kafes*, tiny quarters inside the enclosed harem, where princes were waited on by deaf-mutes and entertained by sterile concubines (mistresses). When a sultan died, he was replaced by one of his brothers taken from the Cage. Many of these men had gone mad from being confined, and power rested with the people who controlled them.

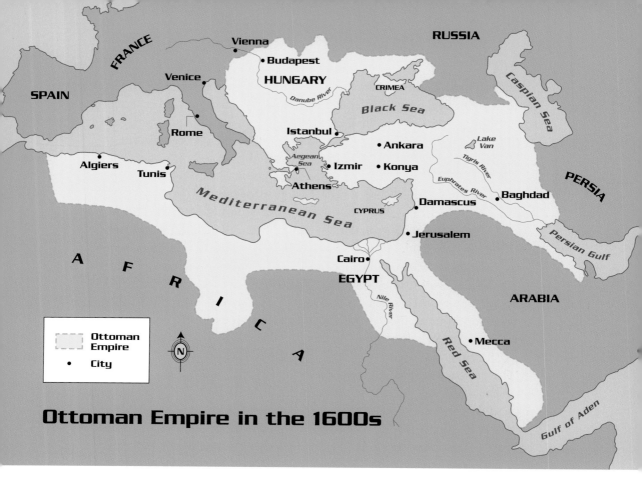

Ottoman Empire in the 1600s

Sultanate of Women. The women of the imperial harem, especially the mother of the sultan, played very influential roles in Ottoman politics. At times, harem women joined forces with military officers to gain influence, for it was believed that whoever could control the sultan could run the state.

In addition to the power of the Janissary Corps and the residents of the seraglio (palace), religious leaders also had strong influence over the affairs of the empire. For example, the entire legal system of the Ottoman Empire was directed by Muslim religious scholars and judges. All laws were in accord with the Quran, which forms the basis of Islamic teaching.

Occasionally, skilled but ruthless administrators, such as the Koprulu family of the seventeenth century, tried to bring order to the poorly run Ottoman royal house. As the Ottoman state tried to reform in the seventeenth and eighteenth centuries, the Islamic establishment became resistant to change. The Janissaries—powerful beyond all control—also opposed new ideas and innovations that would weaken their position. As its European neighbors began to advance in areas of commerce and technology, the Ottoman Empire was hampered by its inflexible traditions and values.

The Fall of the Janissaries and a Weakening Empire

In 1826 Sultan Mahmud II tried to achieve two goals: the elimination of the overly powerful Janissaries and the introduction of Western-style modernization. In order to provoke the Janissaries, Mahmud commanded them to dress and march in Western style. When they rebelled and tried to storm the palace, thousands were killed by troops loyal to the sultan. The remaining Janissaries were exiled.

The violent end of the corps marked the beginning of a reform period in the Ottoman Empire, referred to as the Tanzimat (reorganization), during which Western ideas, laws, and technology were gradually brought into the Ottoman world. Governmental improvements were not enough to halt the gradual decline of the empire, however, as conservatives fearing the loss of tradition refused to modernize.

During the eighteenth and nineteenth centuries, the center of power shifted from the Ottoman Empire to Russia, Great Britain, France, Austria, and other European nations. Aware of the empire's weakened position, Europeans began to refer to it as the Sick Man of Europe. Because the empire did not modernize its army, it had a hard time holding on to its widespread territory. European powers began to help themselves to bits of Ottoman land.

Attempts among European nations to divide the Ottoman Empire became known as the Eastern Question. By 1740 the French had gained extensive Ottoman territories. The Russians demanded control of present-day Romania and the Straits for access to the Mediterranean Sea and the Middle East. In addition, sections within the Ottoman Empire rebelled. Greece, for example, won its independence in a war between 1820 and 1829.

During the nineteenth century, Great Britain and France joined the Ottomans to block Russian expansion during the Crimean War (1854–1856). The defeat of the Russians in Crimea, a peninsula in the Black Sea, temporarily restrained their ambitions to acquire Turkish lands. About twenty years later, however, the Turks engaged in another eastern European war against Russia.

After this second conflict, the Congress of Berlin in 1878 created the independent states of Romania, Bulgaria, Albania, Serbia, and Montenegro, all of which were former territories of the Ottoman Empire. Moreover, the island of Cyprus came under British protection, and other Ottoman provinces were given to Austria. Later, the North African possessions were divided among Britain, France, and Italy.

The decline of the Ottoman Empire provoked a revolution in Istanbul in 1908, led by a group known as the Young Turks. Initially, their aim was to achieve a strong, unified nation by imposing more centralized government directed by a legislature. The fears of traditionalists within the Ottoman Empire and the interference of foreign powers limited the impact of the reforms of the Young Turks. Eventually, the new government became a three-person military dictatorship, which focused on economic and military modernization. The administration of the Young Turks lasted through the twentieth century's first global conflict.

World War I and the Treaty of Sèvres

World War I (1914–1918) broke out in Europe in 1914. Turkish fear of Russia, combined with economic aid from Germany, led to the Ottoman Empire's alliance with the Central powers—Germany, Austria-Hungary, and Bulgaria—in their battle against the Allies, led by Great Britain, France, and eventually the United States.

Among the many bloody battles of World War I was the Gallipoli campaign, an Allied plan to knock the Ottoman Empire out of the war by seizing the Straits and choking Turkey's lines of supply. The attack was a disaster for the Allies, due to Allied blunders and to a vigorous Turkish defense led by a young commander named Mustafa Kemal.

Although the Turks were able to defend their possessions in Anatolia, all of their Middle Eastern holdings were lost during the Arab-British military campaigns of 1917 and 1918. From the Suez Canal region (northeast Africa), the British attacked Palestine (modern-day Israel and part of Jordan) and from Iran they attacked Mesopotamia. The Arabs captured the lands from the east bank of the Jordan River to Damascus. Faced with a worsening military situation, the Turks signed a peace agreement on October 30, 1918.

The Turks had lost 325,000 soldiers in battle and counted more than 2 million civilian casualties. This included more than 1 million Armenians, a Christian ethnic group of eastern Turkey. Fearing that the Armenians would help Christian Russia during the war, the Turks deported and massacred them in enormous numbers.

After the war, Allied leaders sliced up Turkey's territory under the Treaty of Sèvres in 1920. Under the agreement, France would control Lebanon and Syria, and Britain was to be awarded Iraq, Transjordan (present-day Jordan), and Palestine. Greece was to take parts of Thrace and the lands surrounding Smyrna. Italy would get the Antalya region of southwestern Anatolia, and the people of Kurdistan, in northeastern Turkey, were to decide their own future in a regional vote. The

Straits, as well as the finances of Turkey, were to be under European control.

Many Turks, including Mustafa Kemal, refused to accept the treaty settlement. A nationalist movement (devoted to the interests of a nation) developed under Kemal's leadership. He organized military resistance to Greek control of Smyrna. The Turkish War of Independence to hold on to Anatolia began in 1920. Thousands of Greeks and Turks died in hard-fought battles as the Greeks pushed inland almost to Ankara. The Turks drove them back and achieved victory in 1922, with Kemal firmly in command.

The Turks renegotiated the Treaty of Sèvres in 1922. The agreements resulting from the conference at Lausanne, Switzerland, gave back to Turkey all of Anatolia, except the Straits, which remained under Allied control until 1938. The Turks, in turn, agreed to surrender the Arab parts of the Ottoman Empire. Ethnic Greeks in Turkey and ethnic Turks in Greece were required to relocate to their ethnic homelands in a massive population relocation.

◉ Birth of the Republic

Six hundred years of Ottoman rule came to an end when Mustafa Kemal declared the foundation of the Republic of Turkey in the new capital of Ankara on October 29, 1923. Although Turkey had a new constitution and was pledged to democracy, the real power of the government remained in the hands of the dynamic Kemal and his assistants. Kemal, who changed his name to Ataturk in 1928, believed he needed to rule as an authoritarian to ensure the reforms that would prepare the country

Ataturk, the name **Mustafa Kemal** adopted in 1928, means Father of the Turks. Ataturk had ambitious plans for the modernization of Turkey.

HONOR AND DIGNITY FOR WOMEN

Ataturk's vision for a modern Turkey included modern roles for Turkish women. He encouraged other Turks, saying, "Let's be courageous in the matter of women. Let's forget fear. Let's give top priority to giving women honour and dignity." On another occasion, he said, "Women have minds too. Let them show their faces to the world, and see it with their eyes. . . . Don't be afraid. Change is essential."

for full democracy. He was a strong ruler determined to transform the nation from a traditional, outdated ruin into a modern, European-style state. Ataturk's vision remains the guiding principle for Turkey in the twenty-first century, and he remains deeply revered throughout the country.

A series of new laws completely altered Turkish society. The new government was entirely secular and broke the control of Muslim religious leaders. Muslim courts and religious schools were closed down. A law code patterned after Switzerland's legal tradition replaced old Islamic law. People were encouraged to dress in European-style clothes. Women no longer wore veils in public. Ataturk believed in equality for women, and women received the right to vote. Polygamy (having more than one wife) was outlawed. The new regime began many other reforms based on practices in the West, including the use of family names and the introduction of the Latin alphabet, international numerals, and the Gregorian (Western) calendar. Ataturk's visionary ideals were welcome to many, but his removal of Islam from the political realm deeply shocked many Turkish people.

By the time of Ataturk's death in 1938, Turkey had gained its place among the independent nations of the world. Much remained to be done to become a fully functioning democracy, but a solid base had been laid down by Ataturk and his associates. Turkey's return as a stable world power was recognized when the Allies returned control of the Straits to Turkey in 1938.

During World War II (1939–1945), Turkey was determined to remain neutral. This decision placed the country in a difficult position because, before the war, most of its trade had been with Germany. Turkey declared war on Germany on February 23, 1945, mainly to gain acceptance as a charter member of the United Nations (UN), a newly established organization to work for world peace. Turkey also became a member of the North Atlantic Treaty Organization (NATO), which was formed in 1949 by European and North American countries to provide mutual defense.

The Era after World War II

At the end of World War II, Ismet Inonu, Ataturk's successor, and his Republican People's Party decided that Turkey was ready to begin genuine democratic rule. Political opposition developed under the Democrat Party, and in the elections of 1950, the Democrats won by a wide margin. For ten years, under the leadership of Adnan Menderes, the Democrat Party remained in power. But by the mid-1950s, economic difficulties began to arise. When political demonstrations erupted, the Democrats tried to restrain freedom of speech and of the press, as well as to discredit opposition candidates.

After some violent student protests, members of the Turkish army seized control of the government in a military coup on May 27, 1960, and jailed the Democrat Party leaders. Within a year, General Cemal Gursel, leader of the coup, ended the temporary military regime and held elections in accordance with the constitution. In May 1961, he resigned from the army and was elected president.

The Modern Era

The Turkish military, which sees itself as the guardian of Ataturk's secular government, has continued to play a visible role in Turkish politics. In March 1971, after the ruling Justice Party failed to control civilian violence related to economic stresses, the army took control of the situation in a coup and again seized the reins of government in 1980. Democratic elections were held in 1983. During the 1990s, the rise of a fundamentalist political Islam brought new conflicts to the Turkish government. In addition, the Turkish army still poses the threat of intervention. The army especially opposes Kurdish nationalism (aiming for a self-ruling Kurdish nation) and political Islamism, both of which it sees as a threat to national unity. In 1996, three years after her election, Turkey's first woman prime minister, Tansu Ciller, formed a coalition government with Necmettin Erbakan—the head of a party that favored some Islamic reforms. Ciller became the foreign minister, and Erbakan, the prime minister.

Tansu Ciller

Until 2002 Turkey was ruled by several coalition governments that fell apart quickly. Government corruption was common. Finally, in November 2002, a single-party government, the Justice and Development Party (AKP) won the national elections. The AKP had a reputation for honesty, and it won with a huge majority in parliament.

A Muslim party, AKP is far removed from radical Islamism. The AKP strives to govern democratically in a modern state that separates religion and politics. Prime Minister Recep Tayyip Erdogan is dedicated to gaining full membership for Turkey in the EU, a desire shared by the majority of Turks.

Regional Tensions

Turkey, the only Muslim member of NATO and a close ally of the United States, was a member of the U.S.-led coalition of nations that fought against Iraq in the 1990–1991 Gulf War. In March 2003, however, at the beginning of the U.S.-led war to topple Iraqi dictator Saddam Hussein, Turkey's parliament rejected a proposal for U.S. troops to attack Iraq from Turkish soil. This move led to the possibility of the suspension of U.S. economic aid to Turkey, a risk the nation was willing to take because of its concern that the United States might support an independent Kurdish state in northern Iraq. Turkey fears that such a state could revive separatist sentiments among the nation's Kurds. In a compromise agreement, Turkey agreed to let the United States use Turkish airspace to fly troops into Iraq, and transportation routes for supplies of food, fuel, and medicine were open across Turkey. The government also agreed to send peacekeeping

Some **NATO Airborne Warning and Control Systems (AWACS) aircraft** were redeployed from Germany to Turkey in February 2003, in anticipation of the U.S.-led war against Iraq.

troops to Iraq in late 2003, but Iraqi opposition forced the United States to turn down the offer.

Four sets of suicide bombings linked to Osama bin Laden's terrorist network al-Qaeda rocked Istanbul in November 2003. Two synagogues (Jewish sites of worship) and a British bank and consulate were attacked in Turkey's worst terrorist attacks in decades. Sixty-one people were killed and several hundred were wounded. Though most Turks embrace moderate Islam, Turkish militants such as those behind the bombings are at odds with Turkey's pro-Western allegiances, and tensions between the two faces of Islam are among the issues the government must try to resolve in the twenty-first century.

The Government

The Constitution of 1982 states that Turkey is a republic with a parliamentary form of government. The 550 members of the legislative branch, which is called the Grand National Assembly, are elected by civilian voters for five-year terms. The assembly appoints the president, who has a nonrenewable term of seven years. The powers of the president were vastly expanded after 1983. The president can veto constitutional amendments, submit referenda, dissolve the legislature, and call for new elections. The president also selects judges for the nation's military and civilian courts.

The prime minister, who is chosen by the president from among the most influential members of the legislature, is responsible for the daily administration of the government. Cabinet ministers oversee governmental departments. The Council of Ministers is made up of members of the cabinet nominated by the prime minister and appointed by the president. Turkey is divided into eighty-one provinces, which are divided into districts and townships. Each province is headed by a governor, who represents the government, and each province has its own elective council.

THE PEOPLE

A mixture of many ethnic groups, the people of Turkey are known as Turks. Every conquering nation that settled in Turkey has affected the makeup of the population. Hittite, Greek, Persian, Roman, Byzantine, and Seljuk empires have made major contributions to Turkish heritage. Refugees and immigrants continue to shift the identity of Turkey's population. For instance, many Bosnian Muslims fled to Turkey in the early 1990s, after war and mass killings disrupted their region.

Turkey's population exceeds 71 million people and is growing at a rapid annual rate of 1.5 percent. At this rate, the population will be close to 100 million in 2050. About 41 percent of the nation's inhabitants live in rural areas, and many are dependent on subsistence farming. That is, they raise only enough food to feed their families. A steady migration of people seeking employment has come from rural villages to urban areas since 1950. Additionally, Turkey exports many workers. More than 1 million Turkish guest workers reside in Western Europe, primarily in Germany, or in oil-producing Arab nations.

The population density is 306 people per square mile (78.5 people per sq. km), but it is disproportionately distributed around the country. The fertile Aegean and Black Sea regions, which include European Thrace, make up less than 25 percent of the land and contain 45 percent of the population.

Ethnic Groups

National unity was a key component to Ataturk's vision of a stable, modern Turkey. Since then, the government has tried to downplay ethnic, religious, and language differences in order to create a homogeneous (unified), secular, Turkish-speaking society. Censuses no longer count ethnic groups, so population figures for these groups are estimates.

Ethnic Turks make up 80 to 88 percent of Turkey's population. But they are not a homogeneous group. The three main Turkish groups are Anatolian Turks, who historically lived on the Central Plateau; the Rumelian Turks, who are descendants of former Ottoman territories in

GREEKS MEET KURDS IN 401 B.C.

"That night they [the Greek soldiers] spent in the open, among the villages lying above the plain by the River Centritis [E. Tigris] . . . which was the frontier between Armenia and the country of the Kurds. There the Hellenes [Greeks] had time to breathe, delighted to see a plain. The river was distant from the mountains nearly a mile. There they had a happy night, with plenty to eat, talking and talking about the struggles now past. For they had spent seven days passing through the Kurds' country, fighting all the time, and they had suffered worse things than all the [Persian] king . . . did to them. They were quit of all that, they thought, and happily fell asleep."

—Xenophon (431–354 B.C.), *Anabasis: The March Up Country*, Book 4.3

the Balkans; and the Central Asian Turks, who originally came from the Caucasus region, southern Russia, and Central Asia.

The largest minority group in Turkey is the Kurds, with an estimated population of 6 to 12 million. An ancient people from western Asia, the Kurds were among the world's first civilized peoples living in the Fertile Crescent. Sumerian writings from 3000 B.C. mention Kurds, as does the Greek historian Xenophon in 401 B.C. Kurds have traditionally lived in a mountainous region called Kurdistan, which covers parts of southeastern Turkey and parts of Syria, Iraq, and Iran. Many Kurds live much as they have for centuries—farming, herding, and trading. Kurdish society is made up of tribes, which are subdivided into clans, or large family groups, ruled by a chief. Kurds have been migrating to Istanbul and other cities, where they maintain separate neighborhoods. A minority of Kurds has become assimilated into Turkish culture. Most Kurds are Sunni Muslims, as are most ethnic Turks, but about one-third of the Kurds belong to a Shiite Muslim sect called Alevi. Ataturk wanted all people in Turkey to speak Turkish, leading to the suppression of the Kurdish language, but most Kurds still speak their native language.

Kurds struggle for cultural and political rights in their host countries, so some Kurds want Kurdistan to be an independent country. In 1984 the militant Kurdistan Worker's Party (PKK) started an armed insurrection in Turkey, launching guerrilla attacks on government personnel and property. The Turkish government responded with violence and repression. The 1999 arrest of Abdullah Ocalan, the leader of the PKK, brought about a cease-fire. In June 2004, however, the PKK announced an end to the five-year cease-fire.

Traditionally, a married **Kurdish woman** returns to her mother's home for forty days when she has a baby. To learn more about the Kurds and the other peoples of Turkey, go to www.vgsbooks.com for links.

Turkey has an Arab population of approximately one million people. They live mostly in the largely Arab province of Hatay, on the Syrian border, and many have family ties in Syria. Most Arabs in Turkey are farmers and are members of the Shiite sect Alevi, a sect that has been persecuted by Sunni Muslims.

Like the Kurds, the Armenians have also lived in Turkey for thousands of years. A tiny remnant remains of the once large (up to two million people) Armenian community in eastern Anatolia that was decimated in 1915. An estimated forty thousand Armenians live in Turkey, mostly in and around Istanbul, where they practice their traditional Christian faith and maintain a separate ethnic identity. Following the dissolution of the Soviet Union in 1991, the independent country of Armenia was established on Turkey's eastern border, a source of pride to Armenians still in Turkey.

Fewer than twenty thousand Greeks live in Turkey, mostly in Istanbul or islands in the Dardanelles. The Greeks are the remains of a population exchange that took place in 1924. More than one million ethnic Greeks in Turkey and half a million ethnic Turks in Greece, many of whom had lived there for generations, were forced to resettle in their matching ethnic nation in an effort to ensure Turkish-Greece peace.

About the same number of Jews as Greeks remain in Turkey. Most of them are descendants of Sephardic Jews who were expelled from Spain in 1492. Jews and other non-Muslims were allowed to practice their religions in the Ottoman Empire. Most of Turkey's Jewish population moved to Israel after that state was established in 1948.

Language

Turkey once was home to peoples who spoke Indo-European languages, which include Greek and Persian. Turkish is an imported tongue of the Ural-Altaic language group. In the Ottoman Empire, educated people spoke Ottoman Turkish, which was a mixture of Turkish, Arabic (a Semitic language), and Persian. Arabic, the language of the Quran, was the language of religion, while Persian was the artistic and diplomatic language.

Ataturk considered language reform and literacy such an important part of nationalism that he traveled the country with chalk and a blackboard, giving public instruction in the new alphabet.

In the nineteenth century, a movement to simplify and unify the language began. Ataturk continued the movement by pushing for the creation of a language that could unite all Turks in one national identity. He purged Turkish of Arabic and Persian words in 1928, creating a logical and practical language but one that lost touch with its historical literary tradition. He also introduced a Latin-based alphabet, which is far easier than the Arabic alphabet. Because language unity was so important to Ataturk, non-Turkish languages were discouraged or even outlawed for use in public. Turkish is spoken by nearly everyone in Turkey. In isolated areas, such as Kurdistan, local residents still speak their native tongues.

Education

During the Ottoman Empire, little was done to develop a national system of education. Students from families wealthy enough to send their children to school spent long hours learning the difficult Arabic alphabet used in the Turkish language. Schools often stressed memorization of passages from the Quran instead of courses directly related to the modern world. The founders of the Turkish republic realized that if Turkey was to become an industrialized country, its schools would have to be drastically updated.

Ataturk and his followers moved swiftly. For the first time, educational planning was done on a nationwide basis. All connections between public schools and the Muslim religion were broken, and only the government controlled education. One of Ataturk's most striking innovations was to replace the Arabic script with a modified form of the Latin alphabet, in which most European languages are written. This change represented the fact that modern Turkey had turned away from the Middle East and had opened new channels of communication with the West.

One of the great aims of the Turkish government is to wipe out illiteracy by providing free and compulsory primary education for all children. Bringing schooling to every part of the nation is a very ambitious undertaking. In the more remote areas that lack funds, teachers, and supplies, the mountainous terrain further hampers educational efforts. The rapid increase in population has also placed new demands on the educational system.

At the beginning of the twenty-first century, almost 97 percent of children aged six to eleven attended primary school classes. Middle school is compulsory too, but attendance is not well enforced. Attendance drops off to about 60 percent, especially in rural areas, where middle schools are few and children, especially girls, are kept home. Turkish secondary education is free but not compulsory. It provides technical and vocational training, in addition to preparatory courses for those intending to continue to the university level. Turkish universities are located in Istanbul, Ankara, Izmir, and

Students gather outside a **primary school in Istanbul.** Ataturk believed that school uniforms promoted a sense of equality among children.

Erzurum. Graduates from universities, technical schools, and teacher-training colleges lead the constant struggle to further Turkey's industrialization.

The literacy rate—only 10 percent in 1927—has risen to about 87 percent in the twenty-first century, although 17 percent more males than females are literate. Roughly 9.6 million pupils are enrolled in primary schools, more than 2.2 million in secondary schools, and about 1.5 million in institutions of higher learning. Turkey has about twenty-seven public universities along with several hundred additional post-secondary institutions. Istanbul University was founded in 1453 and is the country's largest university, with more than 30,000 students attending.

Health

The governmental Ministry of Health is the largest provider of medical care and preventive health care in Turkey. The salaries of state-employed physicians are low, so many doctors prefer to work in urban centers in higher-paying private practice. Urban areas have the most doctors and the best medical facilities, therefore, and people in rural areas sometimes suffer from preventable diseases because of the shortage of professional care. Medical care in eastern Anatolia is generally only available in provincial capitals. In the early 2000s, only one physician existed for every 1,108 people, and only one hospital bed was available for every 400 people. Turkey is working with the World Health Organization to improve accessibility and quality of health care for citizens in poorer and rural parts of the country.

Large-scale immunization campaigns that began in the mid-1980s have had some success in preventing diseases, such as measles, that affect children. Other programs to combat major infectious disease—such as malaria, tuberculosis, and trachoma (an eye disease)—have achieved progress. Greater availability of safe, drinkable water has led to a decline in waterborne illnesses, especially in diarrhea among children. The official AIDS rate is 0.1 per 100,000. While the number of reported cases of the human immunodeficiency virus (HIV), the virus that often causes acquired immunodeficiency syndrome (AIDS), remains low, international health organizations believe that the prevalence (percentage of the population affected) is rising. Turkey continues to move toward a more equitable model of health care, but the infant mortality rate of 44 deaths in every 1,000 live births is far higher than Europe's. Life expectancy is 69 years of age for men and 74 years for women. About 30 percent of the population is under 15 years of age, and 6 percent is over age 65.

Family planning is encouraged by the government to reduce high birth rates. Islam does not forbid married people from limiting the number of children they have, though religious leaders say Islam does not permit abortion. Abortion, however, is legal in Turkey.

◉ Women and Family Life

Turkey has a larger percentage of women lawyers, doctors, and engineers than many Western nations. Almost 40 percent of young stockbrokers are women. Nonetheless, Turkish society is still largely male-dominated, especially outside the large cities. Until recently, men had the legal right to decide where the family would live, whether or not their wives would hold jobs, and to keep the majority of marital assets in a divorce. A January 2002 law changed all that, giving women equal legal rights in the family and bringing hundreds of years of legal inequality for women to an end.

The extended family continues to play a vital role in Turkish life, even for modern, urban individuals. Family loyalty, family duties, and family honor are strongly held values. Family members take care of each other, emotionally and economically. Children are well loved, and special respect is shown toward elders, both women and men. Families also effectively control a member's social behavior through approval or disapproval of an individual's behavior. This may take extreme and rare forms, including so-called honor killings, the murder of female relatives judged to have damaged the family's moral reputation. The government strictly enforces law in these instances, and Muslim leaders condemn the killings.

Headscarves, the Islamic-style head coverings that traditional Turkish women wear, have become a controversial issue in Turkey. Ataturk rejected head covering as outdated and oppressive of women. It is outlawed in Turkey in government offices, schools, and universities. Yet more than half the women in Turkey, especially those in rural areas, still cover their heads. Emine Erdogan, the prime minister's wife, is one of them. Some young Muslim women are returning to the custom to show their allegiance to Islam. A group of young women in Istanbul marched in 2002 for the right to wear headscarves in school. The headscarf has become a symbol of the struggle to balance nationalism, which wants to keep religion out of politics, with freedom of religious expression.

CULTURAL LIFE

Culture in Turkey blends time and place. Modern music weaves traditional melodies into pop hits, while weavers still produce carpets whose evolution lies in the Turks' central Asian nomadic history. Byzantine Christian churches, classic examples of architecture, still function as places of prayer. The addition of minarets has converted most of them into mosques. Literature expresses contemporary social and political concerns in imaginative forms.

The Arts

Love of abstract pattern and color is a hallmark of Turkish art. Islam discourages representation of humans in art, so Islamic art mastered geometric design, especially patterns based on mathematical formulas. Iznik was the center of tile and ceramic production, and Iznik tiles achieved heights of gracefulness and symmetry. Blue and white tiles, bringing to mind the purity of water and the spaciousness of sky, were produced to line the interiors of palaces and mosques.

Calligraphy (artistic handwriting) also drew on a genius for design, and illuminated Quran manuscripts (decorated in bright inks, including gold and silver) are among the most beautiful works of world art. Even the sultan's signature became an ornate and complex pattern.

Representational art in Turkey before the nineteenth century was primarily found in miniatures—highly colored works painted on small canvasses with exacting detail—which was a tradition imported from Persia. This art form serves as a type of period documentation of the Ottoman Empire. In the twentieth century, Turkey gradually developed new artistic styles, seeking to blend Turkish folk styles with modern art movements, painting about social issues, or exploring abstract painting.

Carpet making is an age-old art for which Turkey is famous. Woven by women, carpets served as portable floor and wall coverings for nomadic families. Extraordinary patterns and rich, warm colors were influenced by tradition and locale, but each

A **carpet weaver** in Selcuk demonstrates how a carpet is crafted.

woman weaver gave her work individuality. Village women still weave carpets to sell. A vibrant craft tradition exists, which is displayed in the bazaars, or street markets, of Turkey's cities. The artisanship of hammered brass and copper, ceramics, jewelry, leatherwork, and inlaid wood remains strong in Turkey.

Architecture

Turkish architectural designs came partially from the Seljuks, whose functional nomadic style evolved slowly as they absorbed Arab and Persian culture. In addition, when the Ottoman Turks conquered the city of Constantinople in 1453, they inherited a rich legacy from the Byzantine Empire. They readily adopted the style of the Hagia Sophia basilica, which had been constructed by the Christian emperor Justinian in the sixth century A.D. The Turks studied and analyzed this place of worship, converted it into a mosque for their own use, and made it the model for most mosques built around Istanbul and other cities of the Ottoman world.

Sinan was the greatest Ottoman architect. He (and other architects who designed mosques) also designed public baths, called *hamams*.

Islam emphasizes personal cleanliness, and these domed structures with marble interiors were popular gathering places. Because women rarely left their homes otherwise, the hamams were important places for them to socialize and exhange news. Women went on separate days from men. Hamams are still open throughout Turkey.

The eighteenth century was called the Tulip Era in architecture because the tulip, Turkey's national flower, was the major design element, especially in tiles. European architectural influence rose to dominance in this era.

After the founding of the Republic of Turkey, new buildings arose in the modernist style, with plain lines and no ornamentation. In the twenty-first century, many Turks live in concrete-block apartments, while old buildings of national heritage are commonly restored and used as hotels, restaurants, and museums.

TURKISH BATH

"I was in a narrow room of marble, with a vaulted roof, and a fountain of warm and cold water; the atmosphere was in a steam, the choking sensation went off, and I felt a sort of pleasure presently in a soft boiling simmer, which, no doubt, potatoes feel when they are steaming."

—William Makepeace Thackeray, (British writer), *Notes of a Journey from Cornhill to Grand Cairo* (1865)

Tiles featuring red tulips were added to the Topkapi Palace decor during the Tulip Era. Go to www.vgsbooks.com for links to websites with more photographs and information about Turkish art, architecture, food, music, and dance.

> Mystic is what
> they call me,
> Hate is my only enemy;
> I harbor a grudge
> against none,
> To me the whole wide world
> is one.
>
> —Yunus Emre
> (CA. 1241–1320), Sufi
> (Islamic mystic)
> Turkish poet

Literature

Ottoman literature flourished in different forms for six hundred years. The courtly, or Divan, school of poetry, with its themes of love, is most famously represented by Fuzuli (CA. 1494–1556). He wrote in Persian and Arabic, considered to be the artistic languages, as well as Turkish. His most famous work is the Middle Eastern favorite, *Leili and Mejnun*, an exploration of love. Religious poetry, especially the spiritual poetry of the Sufis (mystical Islam) is best represented by Mevlana Jalal al-Din Rumi (1207–1273), known simply as Rumi, who wrote in literary Persian. He remains very popular in Turkey and in the West. Folk literature took many forms, including epics, legends, riddles, and poetry. Storytelling—such as the exploits of Karagoz (Black Eyes), a shadow puppet who has many adventures and who outwits his enemies—is still favored in towns and villages. Folk poet Yunus

A Turkish shadow puppet tale may use **colorful shadow puppets** as well as a storyteller. Turkish storytellers traditionally start their tales by saying, "Bir var mis, bir yok mis," meaning, "Maybe it happened, maybe it didn't."

Emre (CA.1241–1320) wrote in vernacular (everyday) Turkish in the thirteenth century and remains a beloved Turkish poet. Like Rumi, he wrote on spiritual themes of universal love and shared humanity.

In the nineteenth century, Tanzimat (reformation) literature developed. This movement introduced European forms: novels, short stories, plays, and essays. Later in the century, nationalist literature—inspired by the writing of Ziya Gokalp—emphasized unity among Turks. It focused on stories, written in clear Turkish, about rural life, urban problems, and social themes.

Writers of the Republican period after 1923 wrote about political and social issues shaped by the ideology of nationalism (an emphasis on the primary importance of a nation's interests and culture). Literary progress was fueled by the introduction of the new alphabet in 1928. Halide Edib was an author of this period who was also a pioneering feminist, educator, and politician. She wrote novels as well as her memoirs. In the 1930s, a new movement in poetry was initiated by Nazim Hikmet, who championed free-form poetry and achieved international fame. The village novel came to prominence in the 1950s and is represented by works such as *Our Village* by Mahmut Makal, which exposed the hardships of rural life in Anatolia. Yasar Kemal, a Kurd, wrote *Mehmet, My Hawk*, a tale of oppression, love, and freedom. This book is among the nation's most popular works and has been translated into more than a dozen languages.

Yasar Kemal

Many women writers came onto the scene starting in the 1970s, including Leyla Erbil, Sevgi Sosyal, and Nazli Eray, among others. Latife Tekin writes in a magic-realism (fairy-tale-like) style about political realities. Her novel *Dear Shameless Death* tells of a family who migrates to the big city. Her work is a best-seller in Turkey and has been translated into several languages.

Other contemporary authors include Bilge Karasu and Orhan Pamuk. One of Turkey's foremost novelists, Pamuk writes in an imaginative and magical style in books such as *The White Castle*, a novel about an Italian slave in seventeenth-century Istanbul. In 1994 Karasu's *Night*, a novel about terror, won the Mobil Corporation's Pegasus Prize honoring works from countries whose literature is rarely translated into English.

A Turkish craftsman in Bursa made the **three-stringed *saz*** he is playing.

Music

Turks love music, and a wide variety of styles are popular. Much Turkish music sounds unfamiliar to foreign ears because it uses a series of quarter tones instead of the whole or half tones of Western scales.

Lively Turkish folk music is still performed in villages, at weddings and festivals. *Ozan* is the music of the *asik,* or folk poets, of Anatolia. It is performed by wandering musicians to the music of the *saz,* a kind of lute with three strings. It is a fading tradition, though the songs are still popular. Kurds have their own folk music, accompanied by haunting wind instruments. *Ozgun,* or protest, music is heard in the cities. The musician Zulfu Livaneli is the best example. Classical music from the Ottoman court is performed by ensembles of more than thirty musicians playing traditional instruments, including the *ney,* a reed flute, and the *tambur,* a long-necked lute. The Mevlani religious order of dervishes, whose members practice a devotional whirling dance, composes a mystical, enchanting music. As many people have moved from villages to big cities, so music has followed, and much Turkish music is traditional folk music interpreted by urban musicians. Music that blends Turkish themes with Western pop is very popular. One of Turkey's best-known pop stars is Tarkan, and Sertab Erener is a popular female vocalist. Erener won the 2003 Eurovision Song Contest, an annual televised competition of European pop singers.

Religion

About 98 percent of Turkey's population are Muslims, but the constitution protects the practice of other religions without interference. Turkey is home to small numbers of Christians, mostly Armenian or Greek, and Jews. Jews and Christians are called People of the Book, since the Bible is considered a sacred book that preceded Islam.

Islam is a monotheistic (one god) religion that arose on the Arabian Peninsula in the seventh century A.D. A Muslim is, literally, "one who submits to God." Islam was instituted by the prophet Muhammad. Muslims believe he received revelations from Allah through the angel Gabriel. These revelations are recorded in elegant Arabic in the holy book of Islam, the Quran. Muhammad is considered the greatest and final prophet through whom God revealed messages. Islam accepts and reveres Jesus Christ and the Jewish prophets of Hebrew Scripture as earlier Islamic prophets but considers itself to be the perfection and completion of the earlier messages.

Islam has split into many sects, but all religious Muslims observe the five pillars of Islam: to declare belief in one God and that Muhammad is God's prophet, to give alms (charity), to fast during the holy month of Ramazan (Ramadan in Arabic), to make a pilgrimage to Mecca at least once if possible, and to pray five times daily. The Islamic ethical code encourages conduct that is generous, fair, chaste, honest, and respectful.

Most Turks are Sunni Muslims, members of the orthodox (conventional) branch of Islam, which traces religious leadership back to the elected caliphs (spiritual heads of Islam) who followed Muhammad. The Shiite sect traces leadership back to members of Muhammad's family. Most Arabs in Turkey, some Kurds, and a small percentage of ethnic Turks are Shiite Muslims.

Since the twelfth century, Turkey has seen the development of a mystical interpretation of Islam called Sufism. Sufis reject materialism and follow a spiritual path emphasizing personal harmony with divine love. Sufi orders are centers of spiritual, social, and political life. They were outlawed by Ataturk but later revived. One example is the Mevlani order, founded by the famous poet Rumi in the thirteenth century. Mevlani members, who engage in a musical whirling ceremony, are known as whirling dervishes. Both women and men follow Sufism, and some of the earliest, famous saints (people honored after their death as especially holy) were women. Folk Islam in Turkey, practiced among rural people, has been heavily influenced by Sufism.

In Turkey the word *masallah* is commonly spoken as a protective shield against bad luck. It means "praise God." *Insallah* means "God willing" and is used to convey that the speaker may wish or hope to do something but acknowledges that, after all, who knows what will happen in the future?

As part of Ataturk's drive to modernize Turkey, he and his associates emphasized rational, scientific thinking over what they considered backward religious traditions. The rapid and nondemocratic establishment of a secular government and the end of public observance of religious traditions—such as the women's veil or headscarf and the connection of Muslim religious leaders with the judicial system—have caused considerable tension among Turks. The government took a more tolerant attitude toward religion in the 1970s and 1980s. Mosque attendance in urban areas, once far lower than in rural areas, had increased considerably by the end of the twentieth century.

Holidays and Festivals

Turks celebrate both religious and secular holidays. New Year's Eve and New Year's Day are popular times to exchange gifts and cards with family and friends. Kurds celebrate the Kurdish New Year, Nowrus (New Day), on March 21 or 22, at the time of the spring equinox, with a bonfire. Observant Muslims celebrate the holy month of Ramazan, the ninth month of the Muslim calendar. The holiday commemorates the time when the prophet Muhammad received his first messages from Allah. During this sacred month, Muslims fast from sunrise to sunset. The evening meal starts with some dates, and a festive meal follows. At the end of the month are three days of celebration and feasting called Seker Bayrami (Sugar Festival). Children receive gifts, and most religious Turkish Muslims try to return home to visit family. Seventy days after Seker Bayrami, Kurban Bayrami (Feast of the Sacrifice) is celebrated. Sheep are slaughtered, and some of the meat is donated to people in need.

Whirling dervishes from the Mevlani order of Sufism demonstrate their sacred dance. Each dancer wears a red felt hat called a fez. It has no brim so that the wearer can put his forehead to the ground in prayer.

Children's Day is April 23. Ataturk established this date to honor children, and Turkey was the first to observe this holiday, which is recognized by the United Nations. It is also the date of Turkey's National Independence Day, the day of the first meeting of Ataturk's Republican Party in Ankara in 1923. Ataturk's death on November 10 is solemnly commemorated with several minutes of silence every year.

Many festivals take place in Turkey throughout the year. The International Film Festival is held in Istanbul in the spring. The Istanbul International Art and Cultural Festival is a chance to see all kinds of Turkish art, music, and dance. It is held every year in June and July. The Cappadocia Wine Festival and the watermelon festival in Diyarbakir are examples of harvest festivals. Greased wrestling in Edirne takes place at the time of the olive harvest, when wrestlers, clad in leather loincloths, grease themselves all over with olive oil. The Mevlana Festival takes place in Konya in December. The festival honors Mevlana Jalal al-Din Rumi, the Sufi poet who was also the founder of the Mevlani order, on the anniversary of his death. The whirling dervishes can be seen performing their sacred dance at this festival.

Food

With its many ethnic, cultural, and climatic influences, Turkey enjoys a wide range of foods. Mediterranean fruits and nuts meet spices that originally came from China and India. In the countryside, cracked wheat bread and creamy yogurt are staples of the local diet. Eggplant

CACIK (CUCUMBER WITH YOGURT AND MINT)

Yogurt was the food of nomadic Turks from early times and remains popular in twenty-first-century Turkey. Serve as a refreshing salad, as a topping for kebabs or sandwiches, or add a few ice cubes to each serving to make a cold soup.

1 cup thick yogurt

1 garlic clove, peeled and minced

1 cucumber, peeled and cut into cubes

¼ cup fresh mint leaves, finely chopped

1 teaspoon salt

½ teaspoon freshly ground black pepper

1. To make thick yogurt, line a mesh strainer with cheesecloth or a paper coffee filter, and set over a large bowl. Spoon the yogurt into the strainer and allow to sit, refrigerated, overnight. Discard the liquid.
2. In a medium bowl, stir together the thick yogurt and garlic with a fork.
3. Add the remaining ingredients and stir until thoroughly mixed together. Refrigerate until used.

Serves 4

(fried, baked, stuffed, or roasted), tomatoes, and kebabs—chunks of meat roasted on a skewer—are found everywhere. Lamb is a favorite meat and turns up in many dishes. A favorite dessert is baklava, which consists of paper-thin, flaky sheets of pastry layered with honey and nuts. Other pastries have descriptive names such as "twisted turban" or "nightingale's nest." Tea plantations are found along the Black Sea, and strong tea is served with sugar cubes all day long throughout the country in little tulip-shaped glasses. Turkish coffee, thick and sweet, is famous from the days when the Ottoman Empire included Arabia, where coffee grows. Strict Muslims drink no alcohol, but alcohol is served in most parts of Turkey. Raki—an anise-flavored, alcoholic drink—is a national drink.

Sports and Recreation

Turks are great recreation enthusiasts, and soccer is their most popular sport. Turks were thrilled when their soccer squad came in third in the 2002 World Cup, Turkey's first World Cup since 1954.

Horses have been a beloved part of Turkish life from the time nomads rode Turkish ponies across the grassy steppes. *Cirit* is a game in which players on horseback going full speed hurl javelins at each other. Turkey also supports avid riding and racing fans. Another sport, greased wrestling, is also a popular event, especially at fairs and festivals. To make the wrestling holds more difficult, participants grease their bodies with olive oil. Camel wrestling matches are held in the province of Aydin.

Turkey has bid three times to host the Olympic Games in Istanbul, the only city which can stage the games on two continents. The Turkish parliament passed the Olympic Act, which ensures permanent funding for sports facilities, and $181 million has already been spent. The Olympic Evaluation Committee considered Istanbul a borderline case in 2001. Ten billion dollars more is slated to be spent, much of it on major transportation projects, including a Bosporus Tunnel, before reapplying in 2012.

Turks are fond of relaxing at excellent beaches along the country's thousands of miles of seacoast. During leisure hours, many Turkish men play backgammon, an ancient board game, in local coffeehouses.

THE ECONOMY

By the early twenty-first century, Turkey had made impressive strides toward industrial modernization. Manufacturing dominates much of the economy, and Turkey exports manufactured goods throughout the region. Agriculture is strong, and Turkey is one of the few countries in the world that is self-sufficient in food. The nation is struggling with a high rate of inflation. In the early part of the century, the inflation rate rose 45 percent—a trend that hurts consumers as well as businesses. To combat inflation, the government has cut its budget and sold many of its state-owned businesses. In 1996 Turkey entered into a customs-union agreement with the European Union, which allows the nation to trade with EU members on favorable terms. But the government still faces an uphill battle in bringing the country's wages and prices under control.

Agriculture

Agriculture employs 40 percent of Turkey's workers while providing 13 percent of the gross domestic product (GDP), a measure of the nation's

economic output. New seeds, new farming techniques, and irrigation projects from major dam projects have successfully increased crop yields. As a result, Turkey not only is one of the few nations in the world that is self-sufficient in food but it is also a food exporter. About 95 percent of all Turkish farm families own their own land, and the average farm covers 12 acres (5 hectares).

Turkey's varying climates allow the cultivation of a wide array of crops. In the autumn, Anatolian farmers sow wheat and barley that ripen the following summer, and apple and cherry trees produce fruit for the fall harvest period.

The chief commercial crops are tobacco and cotton, which are grown in many districts. Tobacco production is centered in Izmir on the Aegean Sea and Samsun on the Black Sea. High yields of cotton are found mainly near Adana, a flat southern area ideal for mechanized cultivation.

Dried figs and raisins are produced in the hot western valleys and are exported through the port of Izmir. Apricots and grapes appear in many areas nationwide, and orange trees flourish along the southern coast. Olives come mainly from the mountainous regions to the south, and the annual harvest of nuts—including pistachios, almonds, and high-quality hazelnuts—is of national agricultural importance.

Livestock raising fits well into the general farming pattern. Sheep, goats, and cattle are the most profitable animals to raise. Wool is a significant export. The country's population of Angora goats is a natural source of mohair, an expensive fabric or yarn that is silky, fluffy, and strong. Angora is a variation of the name Ankara, and the goats are raised on the central plain south of the capital city.

Mining and Fishing

Turkey holds a rich variety of mineral deposits, yet they remain largely untapped. Lack of funds and a shortage of processing plants have hampered the growth of the nation's potentially valuable mining industry. Mining contributed about 2 percent of the GDP in the late twentieth century.

Coal is used for fuel in steel mills (factories). The largest coalfield, at Zonguldak on the Black Sea, is the only substantial deposit in southwestern Asia. Turkey is also one of the world's principal producers of chromite, from which chrome is made. The ore comes mostly from Guleman on the nation's southeastern coast. Iron ore is mined at Divrigi. Meerschaum is mined in Eskisehir in northwestern Anatolia. This ivorylike, soft, white mineral is carved into tobacco pipes and jewelry by Turkish craftworkers. Petroleum is found in the southeastern part of the country, and natural gas is found in the basin of the Sea of Marmara. Turkey imports most of its oil and gas, however. Pipelines for the transportation of oil and gas are controversial issues in Central Asia and the Middle East because of economic, environmental, and political tensions. Iraq exported much of its oil through Turkey until the UN imposed sanctions on Iraq after the 1991 Gulf War. Closure of Iraqi pipelines has cost Turkey millions of dollars in pipeline fees as well as loss of domestic supply. Furthermore, large-scale smuggling of Iraqi oil into Turkey has cost the government large amounts of lost taxes.

A **fish market in Taksim,** a suburb of Istanbul, sells many varieties of seafood.

Despite its access to three important seas, Turkey has only a modest fishing industry. Based in the Straits, fishers take advantage of fish migrations from the Black Sea to the Mediterranean. Anchovies make up the largest part of the catch, which in the mid-1990s was about 600,000 tons (544,370 metric tons) annually.

Manufacturing and Industry

Since 1980 Turkey has established an increasingly diverse and sophisticated industrial base, aided by loans from the United States and the International Monetary Fund (IMF). Industry accounts for 30 percent of the GDP.

In the early 2000s, manufacturing in Turkey focused on consumer goods, food processing, and on the production of textiles that used locally produced cotton. The mill at Kayseri, for example, is the largest textile producer in the Middle East. The textile and clothing industry employs about one-fifth of Turkey's industrial workers and makes up almost 40 percent of Turkey's export sales. Most factories are located in and around the large cities of northern and western Turkey.

Iron- and steel-producing plants are concentrated on the coast of the Black Sea. Turkey has had one of the fastest growing iron and steel industries in the world. The steel complex at the port of Iskenderun on the Mediterranean has an estimated annual output of 2 million tons (2.03 million metric tons). Cement production for the construction industry has continued to increase in the early 2000s, reflecting increased infrastructure (especially highways and dams) and housing projects.

Turkey used to be one of the primary manufacturers of illegal opium (a narcotic), but since 1974, the government has effectively maintained strict control over legal opium poppy processing. Turkey, however, lies between the great opium production centers of Pakistan and Afghanistan and is a key transit route. Despite government attempts to control the traffic, opium gum, morphine base, and heroin are still smuggled through Turkey.

Service Sector

The service sector of Turkey's economy has grown to account for more than half the workers in the country and 55 percent of the GDP. This sector includes jobs in education, health care, retail sales, transportation, trade, and tourism. Government jobs have developed significantly, but this sector is often burdened by inefficiency. Banking also employs many service workers. The Central Bank of Turkey is responsible for issuing banknotes and overseeing currency, as well as regulating the banking system and credit.

By the end of the twentieth century, tourism had developed into a major source of foreign currency for Turkey. Since then, however, the tourist economy in Turkey has been troubled by political and environmental problems. Once drawing an annual total of about 7 million visitors spending an estimated $4.3 billion each year, Turkey's tourist economy has been devastated by fears of earthquakes, the 2003 war in Iraq, and terrorism on Turkish soil.

When regional tensions are less prominent, tourists come to Turkey to see Istanbul's historic buildings, mosques, and art treasures. In addition, Turkey's ancient ruins—at Troy, Pergamum, Ephesus, and elsewhere— bring interested people from around the world. Moreover,

The ornate Library of Celsus is one of the sights to see among 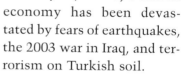 **the ruins at Ephesus.** They are from the ancient Roman Empire.

There is room for more sunbathers on this beach in Bodrum. This city is also a popular departure point for holiday cruises on the Mediterranean Sea.

the coastal areas on the Aegean and Mediterranean seas appeal to both Turks and foreign visitors as places to enjoy the warm climate. These areas are far from troubled borders. Sailing trips along the coasts are magnificent. Ski resorts in the Northwest also draw seasonal crowds.

Unemployment

One of the biggest difficulties in recent Turkish history has been unemployment. During the late 1970s, unemployment was among the causes of community violence, which contributed to the 1980 military coup. The unemployment rate in the early twenty-first century is 11 percent, down from 17 percent in 1985.

The unemployment figure would be much higher if not for the more than one million Turks who work abroad—mostly in Germany and the Middle East. For Turks who work in Europe, the situation is often very difficult. Most foreign workers leave their families at home, and when European economies decline, Turkish laborers are the first to be laid off. Even so, workers sent home close to $3 million each year. Turkey's average yearly income per person is $2,610.

ILLEGAL IMMIGRANTS

Istanbul is a gateway to illegal entry into Europe for many immigrants from Africa, Afghanistan, Bangladesh, northern Iraq, and other places. Smugglers in Turkey conduct an organized and efficient business, using mobile phones to stay in touch with smugglers around the world. Migrants pay for transport on boats that run regularly from Istanbul to Italy and Greece, countries with long, hard-to-patrol coastlines. The Turkish government struggles to patrol its own long coastline and rugged land borders, a very costly operation.

The **Ataturk Dam and Hydroelectric Power Plant,** the centerpiece of the Southeast Anatolia Project (GAP), is pictured on the 1 million Turkish lira banknote (paper money). The dam was completed in a little over four years, a world record in construction time. It began generating electricity in 1992.

Energy and Transportation

Although Turkey can produce some oil, its industrial and economic growth still suffers from lack of fossil fuels. About half of the electrical energy generated in the nation comes from hydroelectric plants. The Keban Dam on the upper Euphrates near Elazig has produced power for years. In 1992 the even larger Ataturk Dam began operation on the lower Euphrates.

With German aid, the Ottoman sultans of the nineteenth century built the first Turkish railroads, which connected Istanbul with Paris via the famous Orient Express line. By the time of World War I, railroads linked all parts of the Ottoman Empire to Istanbul and reached other Middle Eastern capitals. After independence in 1923, a government-owned railway network emerged. In the twenty-first century, the Turkish Republic State Railways are perhaps the best in the Middle East.

An excellent highway system, which is connected to Europe by the Bosporus Bridge, supplements the railways. Turkey has 237,400 miles (382,048 km) of national highways, of which 66,471 miles (106,976 km) are paved. About 4 million motor vehicles are registered, including 3 million cars and 100,000 buses.

Turkey has 120 airports. Istanbul's busy airport handles international traffic, while Ankara is the major center for travel within Turkey. Turkish Airlines offers international service from both Istanbul and Ankara, as well as regularly scheduled domestic flights.

Istanbul on the Bosporus and Izmir on the Aegean Sea are the main seaports. They have become increasingly and dangerously crowded in recent times. Modernizing schemes have included upgrading the facilities at Izmir and constructing a port east of Tekirdag on the Sea of Marmara—estimated to be completed in 2015—intended to relieve Istanbul's seaside congestion. Black Sea ports, such as Samsun, Sinop, and Trabzon, have good services, but their location means they also attract less traffic. Internal shipping is limited, as few of Turkey's rivers are navigable.

◉ The Future

Turkey holds the allure of bridging the Western world with the world of the Middle East and the Christian world with the Islamic world. A strong democracy in an Islamic nation has much to offer a troubled region facing the redevelopment of Iraq after the wars of 1990–1991 and 2003. Yet the challenges that Turkey faces in the early 2000s are complex. Twice since 1960, military coups have toppled the government, and the military continues to consider itself the guardian of Ataturk's legacy. The rise of Islam as a political force could affect this strongly secular government. Turkey strives to maintain the fine balance between the democratic process and the separation of religion, the military, and politics. Confronted with economic difficulties, including high unemployment and a large foreign debt, Turkish politicians must also be alert to widespread economic crises and to the social problems that often follow. The PKK, the Kurdish separatist group, ended its cease-fire in 2004. Continued unrest is possible if minority rights are not consistently enforced. Moreover, tensions between Greeks and Turks continue, and conflict in neighboring Iraq creates additional strain on regional relations. These threats of instability place great stress on the political system and place Turkey's acceptance as a full member of the European Union in question. Drawing on their magnificent past to face their economic and domestic troubles, as well as regional instability, Turks view their nation's future with cautious optimism.

 Stop by www.vgsbooks.com for links to read the latest news about Turkey.

Timeline

CA. 6500 B.C. Neolithic people at Catalhoyuk, Anatolia, establish what may be the world's first urban settlement.

CA. 1750 B.C. The Hittite Empire in Anatolia reaches its peak.

CA. 1200 B.C. Hattusas, the Hittite capital, is destroyed by Phrygians. About the same time, the city of Troy is destroyed. Phrygian, Lydian, and Greek cultures spread in Anatolia.

546 B.C. Persian conquest of Anatolia defeats Croesus, the last ruler of the kingdom of Lydia.

334 B.C. Alexander the Great destroys the Persian Empire in Anatolia.

138 B.C. Anatolia becomes part of the Roman Empire.

CA. A.D. 48–56 Saint Paul spreads Christianity in his missionary travels through Turkey.

326 Emperor Constantine moves the capital of the Roman Empire to the city of Byzantium and renames it Constantinople.

532 The Christian church Hagia Sophia, a masterpiece of Byzantine architecture, is built in Constantinople under the orders of the Byzantine emperor Justinian.

CA. 600s Islam spreads through the Arab world and into Anatolia.

CA. 900s Turks from central Asia begin to arrive in Anatolia and adopt Islam as their religion.

1100s The Sultanate of Rum, a kingdom established by the Seljuk Turks, seizes political control over most of Anatolia from the faltering Byzantine Empire.

1200s Ertugrul becomes the local ruler in northwestern Anatolia and founds the Ottoman dynasty. The Ottomans quickly erode Seljuk and Byzantine power.

1204 Constantinople is sacked by members of the Fourth Crusade, an armed Christian religious pilgrimage from Western Europe.

1261 Byzantine government regains control of Constantinople.

1345 Ottoman Turks gain their first European foothold when Orhan I crosses the Dardanelles from Anatolia into Thrace.

1453 The conquest of Constantinople on May 29 by the Ottoman Turks signals the end of the Byzantine Empire and the establishment of the Ottomans as a great Islamic empire. The city is renamed Istanbul.

1520–1566 The reign of Suleyman the Magnificent sees the expansion of the Ottoman Empire into the most powerful empire in the world.

CA. 1520s–1600s The power of the sultans declines during an era known as the Sultanate of Women. Members of the Janissary Corps and of the harem come to have great political power in the court at Topkapi Palace.

1740   The French gain extensive Ottoman lands, as European nations rise in power and the Ottoman Empire weakens.

1826   The Janissary Corps rebels against the Western-style modernizations of Sultan Mahmud II. The Janissaries are executed or exiled, and a reform period, known as the Tanzimat, begins.

1854–1856   Britain and France join the Ottomans fighting against Russia in the Crimean War.

1878   The Congress of Berlin creates the independent states of Romania, Bulgaria, Albania, Serbia, and Montenegro out of former Ottoman territories.

1908   A group known as the Young Turks revolts against the Ottoman government, desiring to create a Western-style unified government. The new government becomes a three-person military dictatorship with the sultan as the nominal head of government.

1915   More than one million ethnic Armenians in Turkey are killed during a mass deportation by the Turkish government. Turkey defends its control of the Straits at Gallipoli.

1920   The Turkish government signs the Treaty of Sèvres with the Allies, which reduces Turkey to Istanbul and part of Anatolia.

1923   Mustafa Kemal Ataturk declares the foundation of the Republic of Turkey in the new capital of Ankara.

1945   Turkey declares war on Germany in February to become a charter member of the newly formed United Nations at the end of World War II.

1960   The Turkish army seizes control of the government in a military coup.

1961   Democratic national elections are held.

1974   Turkey invades the island of Cyprus and occupies one-third of it.

1980   The Turkish army seizes control of the government for the third time.

1983   Elections for a civilian government are held. Prime Minister Turgut Ozal and General Kenan Evren are the leaders of the new government.

1999   Abdullah Ocalan, the leader of the Kurdish separatist group, the PKK, is captured in February. In August an earthquake kills more than twenty thousand people in the area of Izmit and Istanbul.

2003   An earthquake in the Bingol area of eastern Turkey kills 115 people. Turkish militants with links to al-Qaeda carry out four sets of bombings in Istanbul.

2004   Cyprus Greeks vote down a UN plan to reunify Cyprus. The PKK announces the end of a cease-fire.

COUNTRY NAME Republic of Turkey

AREA 300,948 square miles (779,455 sq. km)

MAIN LANDFORMS Istranca, Pontic, and Taurus mountains; Gallipoli Peninsula; Central Plateau (Anatolian Plain); Eastern Highlands; Cukur Ova Plain; Arabian Platform

HIGHEST POINT Mount Ararat, 16,949 feet (5,166 m) above sea level

LOWEST POINT Mediterranean Sea (sea level)

MAJOR RIVERS Euphrates (Firat), Tigris (Dicle), Buyukmenderes, Sakarya, Kizil

ANIMALS Anatolian leopards, bears, deer, flamingos, loggerhead turtles, monk seals, wild boar, wolves

CAPITAL CITY Ankara

OTHER MAJOR CITIES Istanbul, Izmir, Adana

OFFICIAL LANGUAGE Turkish

MONETARY UNIT Turkish lira (TL). 1 Turkish lira = 100 kurus.

Currency Fast Facts

TURKISH CURRENCY

The Turkish lira (TL) is the Turkish unit of currency. Coins come in 25,000, 50,000, and 100,000 amounts. Banknotes come in amounts of 250,000, 500,000, 1 million, 5 million, and 10 million lira. Coins come in denominations of 500, 1,000, 2,500, and 5,000 lira. High inflation has made the currency weak, and the cost of a small item may be millions of lira. The government has plans to revalue the currency and drop some zeros.

Turkey adopted its flag in 1936. Sitting in a field of scarlet red, a vertical, white crescent moon opens toward a white, five-pointed star. The moon and star were once both Roman and Christian symbols, but they became associated with Islam in the fifteenth century. Red represents the Ottoman Empire.

The Turkish national anthem, "Istiklal Marsi" ("March of Independence") was officially adopted in 1921 by the Turkish Grand National Assembly. The lyrics were written by the poet Mehmet Akif Ersoy. The council could not meet to choose music until 1924 because of the War of Independence. Eight years after that, in 1932, the music was changed to a composition by Osman Zeki Ungor, conductor of the Presidential Symphonic Orchestra. Below are the anthem's lyrics.

March of Independence

Fear not and be not dismayed, this crimson flag will never fade.
It is the last hearth that is burning for my nation,
And we know for sure that it will never fail.
It is my nation's star, shining forever,
It is my nation's star and it is mine.

Frown not, fair crescent, for I am ready to die for you.
Smile now upon my heroic nation, leave this anger,
Lest the blood shed for thee be unblessed.
Freedom is my nation's right,
Freedom for us who worship God and seek what is right.

For a link to a site where you can listen to Turkey's national anthem, "March of Independence," visit www.vgsbooks.com.

MUSTAFA KEMAL ATATURK (1881–1938) Born in Salonika, Ottoman Empire (modern-day Thessaloniki, Greece), the son of a minor official, Ataturk became the founder of the Republic of Turkey and remains highly revered in Turkey. He was a radical modernizer and Westernizer. Ataturk said he believed in democracy, but he ruled as a dictator and, in pursuit of national unity, suppressed ethnic diversity. An ardent nationalist, he removed religion from politics, saying that religion caused division. He is criticized by some for the ongoing tension this caused in Turkish society. He was a proponent of mutual respect between East and West and between men and women.

TANSU CILLER (b. 1946) Tansu Ciller was Turkey's first woman prime minister, serving from 1993 to 1996. She was born in Istanbul and received her Ph.D. in economics from Yale in the United States. A member of parliament, Ciller leads the True Path Party, a right-of-center party.

HALIDE EDIB (1883–1964) Edib was born in Istanbul and became a leader of the women's emancipation movement in Turkey. She was an associate of Ataturk during the War of Independence. In 1926 she wrote *Memoirs of Halide Edib* in English to explain why she had joined the nationalist movement. She dedicated herself to the improvement of education for women and girls and became head of the English Department at Istanbul University. She was a member of parliament but gave up politics and devoted herself to writing novels.

YUNUS EMRE (CA. 1238–CA.1320) Yunus Emre was a Sufi, born a peasant in a village in Anatolia. Not much is known of his life. He is a poet who wrote in the Turkish language of his own people, rather than the Arabic or Persian languages of the elite. His poetry celebrates Allah's all-embracing love for humanity, which makes all people brothers and sisters.

RECEP TAYYIP ERDOGAN (b. 1954) Erdogan, the leader of the Justice and Development Party, became Turkey's prime minister in 2002. Born in the city of Rize on Turkey's Black Sea coast, he came from a poor background and became the mayor of Istanbul in 1994. He is one of Turkey's most popular politicians, with a reputation for honesty. A committed Muslim, Erdogan served four months in jail for reading a pro-Islamist poem in public. However, he is a pro-Western conservative who wants to bring Turkey into the European Union.

SERTAB ERENER (b. 1964) Born in Istanbul, Erener is one of Turkey's most popular female vocalists. In 1999 she recorded a duet with Ricky Martin, the Latin pop star, called "Private Emotion." In 2003 she won the Eurovision Song Contest with "Every Way that I Can."

NAZIM HIKMET (1902–1963) Like Ataturk, Hikmet was born in Salonika. He became the first poet of the Turkish republic to write in colloquial Turkish, saying, "I want to write poems that talk of a single apple, of the plowed earth, of the psyche of someone getting out of prison, of the struggle of the masses for a better life, of one man's heartaches." A Communist, Hikmet was imprisoned in Turkey for his political beliefs and then lived in exile in the Soviet Union until he died. He is internationally recognized as the foremost modern Turkish poet.

HANDAN IPEKCI (b. 1956) Ipekci is a Turkish film director, born in Ankara, whose 2001 film *Big Man, Small Love* (released internationally as *Hejar*) was Turkey's nomination for Best Foreign Film at the U.S. Academy Awards that year. Ipekci says her film is about creating respect and tolerance in a diverse society. However, it was briefly banned in Turkey because the story of a five-year-old Kurdish girl who wins the heart of a retired Turkish judge raises Kurdish issues controversial in Turkey.

MEHMET II (1432–1481) Mehmet was the seventh sultan in the Ottoman dynasty. He was called Mehmet the Conqueror after he captured Constantinople in 1453. On the evening of the conquest, Mehmet took part in prayers in Hagia Sophia, having had it turned into a mosque immediately. He rebuilt the city into the Ottoman capital of Istanbul. He allowed religious freedom and emphasized just tax and administration systems. Under his rule, the Ottoman Empire expanded from Anatolia westward to the Danube River in Europe.

HAKAN SUKUR (b. 1971) In Turkey called the King, Sukur was born in Adapazari, Turkey, and is the nation's best-known soccer player. Tall and quick, he is a top scorer, averaging a goal every two games. In 2002 he scored the fastest-ever goal in a World Cup game. The same game clinched Turkey's third place in its first World Cup since 1954.

LEYLA ZANA (b. 1961) Born in Bahce, a small village near Diyarbakir in eastern Turkey, Zana became the first Kurdish woman elected to parliament. She was elected in 1991, and in 1994 authorities arrested her and five other Kurdish legislators. They were sentenced to fifteen years in prison for statements made in support of a peaceful resolution to the Kurdish situation. The European Court of Human Rights ruled that her trial was unfair. After ten years of imprisonment, she was released in 2004. She has been awarded many international peace prizes and was nominated for a Nobel Peace Prize for her struggle for human rights and democracy.

ANKARA Ankara has a long history, dating back to the Hittites. The excellent Museum of Anatolian Civilizations there has displays on early peoples. Several significant ruins, including the Column of Julian, represent the time of Roman rule. Remains of Byzantine rule can be seen at the Ankara Kalesi (Castle), where there is also a restoration of a Turkish village. Ataturk chose the city to be the capital of Turkey, and his monumental tomb, the Anit Kabir, is visited by many. Government is the main business of Ankara, and visitors can tour the Presidential Palace and the Grand National Assembly.

CAPPADOCIA The region of Cappadocia, once the center of the Hittite Empire, was formed by volcanoes. Over millions of years, erosion created a moonlike landscape with curious formations called fairy chimneys, columns with boulders perched on top. Humans carved caves out of the soft rock too, and the area is full of early Christian cave churches. The frescoes (wall paintings) decorating the churches are important examples of Byzantine art. They can be seen at Goreme Valley Open-Air Museum.

EPHESUS Ephesus is one of the best-preserved ancient cities in the Mediterranean. As a Greek city, it was the site of the temple of Artemis, one of the Seven Wonders of the World. Ephesus became an important Roman trading town, and Saint Paul visited in the 60s A.D. Visitors can walk past temples, baths, and marble carvings, and visit the Great Theatre, which is still used for performances.

GALLIPOLI The site of major World War I battles, Gallipoli is the peninsula on the northwestern side of the Dardanelles, which guards the entrance to the Straits. The Allied fleet fought to take Gallipoli and failed. Visitors can tour the significant battle sites at the Gallipoli National Historic Park.

ISTANBUL Istanbul is one of the great cities of the world, rich with historical sights. The Roman Hippodrome was the sight of horse races. Hagia Sophia is now a museum. The Blue Mosque was built in Ottoman times to rival Hagia Sophia. Topkapi Palace was the home of the sultan and his court. The Grand Bazaar dates from the 1400s and is made up of four thousand shops where you can buy everything from sheepskin to spices. A boat trip on the Bosporus allows visitors to see the city from the water.

KONYA This city is 31 miles (50 km) from Catalhoyuk, the site of the oldest known human settlement. Mevlana Jalal al-Din Rumi, the great Sufi mystic poet and founder of the Mevlani order, lived here. In modern times, the former lodge of the order's whirling dervishes is the Mevlana Museum. Many people visit it as a holy place. The Festival of Mevlana, held in December, includes dances by whirling dervishes.

coup: the sudden overthrow, often violent, of a government by a small group

delta: a triangular, fertile area of land where one or more rivers spread out into several outlets

dervish: a member of a mystical Islamic religious order dating back to the thirteenth century. Whirling dervishes dance to reach an ecstatic state of unity with the divine.

gross domestic product (GDP): the value of the goods and services produced by a country over a period of time, such as a year

harem: the private, secluded part of a house for women and their attendants and children in a Muslim household

hydroelectric power: electricity produced by the power of rushing water. Dams are built on rivers in order to create hydroelectric power stations.

irrigation: a system of supplying water to agricultural fields using canals, pipes, reservoirs, and other artificial devices

Islam: a religion founded in Arabia in the seventh century A.D. and based on the prophet Muhammad's teachings. Islam's holy book is the Quran.

Janissaries: infantry (foot soldiers) recruited by the practice of forcing Christian children to serve in the sultans' administration or infantry in the Ottoman era

literacy: the ability to read and write

mosque: an Islamic building used for public worship

nationalism: loyalty or devotion to a nation with an emphasis on the promotion of the nation's interests above all things

Persian: the language or people of Persia (modern Iran)

political Islamism: the movement to create an Islamic state, in which the religion is not separate from the state and the law of the country is Islamic law

Quran: the holy book of Islam. The writings of the Quran were set forth by the prophet Muhammad starting in 610 A.D. Muslims believe Allah revealed these writings to Muhammad.

Shiite: a member of one of the two major Islamic sects. Shiites believe that only direct descendants of Muhammad's family are legitimate Islamic rulers.

strait: a channel of water connecting two bodies of water

subsistence farming: a system of farming that produces only enough or not quite enough food necessary to feed the farm family, without any left over for sale

Sufi: a Muslim mystic, or person who believes an individual can have direct knowledge of God

sultan: the king or ruler of a Muslim state

Sunni: a member of one of the two major Islamic sects. Sunnis believe that Muhammad's successors can be chosen from among his closest colleagues and not necessarily from his direct relations.

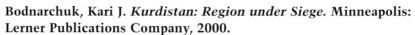

Selected Bibliography

Bodnarchuk, Kari J. *Kurdistan: Region under Siege*. Minneapolis: Lerner Publications Company, 2000.
This title examines in detail the situation of the Kurds in Turkey, Iraq, Iran, and Syria.

Brosnahan, Tom, Pat Yeale, and Richard Plunkett. *Turkey*. Victoria, Australia: Lonely Planet, 2001.
What to see in Turkey and why to bother—Lonely Planet guidebooks cover the practical aspects of travel as well as giving loads of interesting background information.

***The Economist*. 2004.**
<http://www.economist.com> (June 16, 2004)
This weekly British magazine, available on-line or in print editions, provides excellent in-depth coverage of Turkey's economic and political news.

Goodwin, Jason. *Lords of the Horizons: A History of the Ottoman Empire*. New York: Henry Holt, 1998.
The author of this book is a travel writer, as well as a historian and a journalist, and this book reads like a trip through six hundred years of flavorful history. Shadow puppets, Persian poetry, and murderous sultans share pages with descriptions of clothing and architecture.

Gore, Rick. "Wrath of the Gods: Earthquake in Turkey." *National Geographic*, July 2000.
Photographs and charts illustrate this in-depth look at the history and geology of earthquakes in Turkey and how they have shaped the land and the culture of the country.

Kinzer, Stephen. *Crescent & Star: Turkey between Two Worlds*. New York: Farrar, Straus and Giroux, 2001.
Kinzer is a journalist for the *New York Times*. This book is a personal look at contemporary Turkey, reporting on the author's diverse experiences, such as being arrested by Turkish soldiers and enjoying smoking a hookah (water pipe).

Lloyd, Seton. *Ancient Turkey: A Traveller's History*. Berkeley: University of California Press, 1989.
A travel guide and a history book, this well-illustrated volume moves from the prehistoric Anatolia of 8000 B.C. to the travels of Saint Paul in the first century A.D., covering the many cultures in between. The author was the director of the British Institute of Archaeology at Ankara.

Mango, Andrew. *Ataturk: The Biography of the Founder of Modern Turkey*. New York: Overlook Press, 1999.
This is the biography of the complex statesman who transformed a defeated empire into the modern nation of the Republic of Turkey. Maps and photographs round out an in-depth look at Ataturk's life and times.

***The Middle East and North Africa, 2003*. London: Europa Publications, 2003.**
The article on Turkey covers physical and social geography, history, economy, and a broad statistical survey.

Population Reference Bureau. October 20, 2003.
<http://www.prb.org> (June 15, 2004).
The Population Reference Bureau provides demographics on Turkey's population, health, environment, employment, family planning, and more.

Streissguth, Tom. *Cyprus: Divided Island.* Minneapolis: Lerner Publications Company, 1998.
A look at the roots of the conflict that keeps Greek and Turkish Cypriots apart, what the positions are, and what is being done to resolve the situation.

Wood, Michael. *In Search of the Trojan War.* Berkeley: University of California Press, 1996.
The mound of Hisarlik in Turkey is considered to be the site of the ancient city of Troy, where the Trojan War possibly took place in the thirteenth century B.C. Wood looks at the archaeological, literary, and historic evidence in this interesting and nicely illustrated book.

The World Factbook. August 1, 2003.
<http://www.cia.gov/cia/publications/factbook/geos/tu.html> (June 15, 2004).
This site provides ample facts and figures on Turkey's geography, government, economy, communications, transportation, and transnational issues.

"Yunus Emre, Selected Poems." *Republic of Turkey, Ministry of Foreign Affairs.* N.d.
<http://www.mfa.gov.tr/grupe/eg/eg23/01.htm> (June 15, 2004).
A history and critical reading of one of Turkey's greatest poets is found in this in-depth look at Yunus Emre, the mystic Islamic poet from thirteenth century Anatolia.

Bagdasarian, Adam. *Forgotten Fire.* **New York: Random House, 2000.**
The story of the brutal destruction of the world of Turkish Armenians in 1915 is told in this novel for young adults. It is based on the childhood experiences of the author's great-uncle.

Bator, Robert. *Daily Life in Ancient and Modern Istanbul.*
Minneapolis: Runestone Press, 2000.
This book follows the development of Istanbul's personality from its beginning as a fishing village, through the Byzantine and Ottoman empires, to the end of the twentieth century.

BBC News.
<http://news.bbc.co.uk>
The World Edition of the BBC news is updated throughout the day, every day. It is a great resource for up-to-date comprehensive news coverage of Turkey and its neighbors.

Cornell, Kari, and Nurcay Turkoglu. *Cooking the Turkish Way.*
Minneapolis: Lerner Publications Company, 2004.
Find out more about Turkish cooking and Turkish food traditions. Cook your own popular Turkish dishes too, with this volume from the Easy Menu Ethnic Cookbook series.

Dalokay, Vedat. *Sister Shako and Kolo the Goat: Memories of My Childhood in Turkey.* **Translated by Guner Ener. New York: Lothrop, Lee & Shepard, 1994.**
Dalokay grew up in a small Turkish village and became the mayor of Ankara. This is the tale of his boyhood friendship with Sister Shako, an eccentric widow who keeps goats, including the almost human Kolo.

Hicyilmaz, Gaye. *Against the Storm.* **London: Faber and Faber, 1998.**
Inspired by a true story, this novel for young adults is about how Mehmet learns to survive on the streets of Ankara when he and his family are forced to leave their village and how he plans to escape to a better life.

Hikmet, Nazim. *Poems of Nazim Hikmet.* **Translated by Randy Blasing and Mutlu Konuk. New York: Persea Books, 1994.**
The poems of the widely known and revolutionary Turkish poet who wrote in conversational freestyle verse are recognized as among the great poetry of the twentieth century.

Katz, Samuel M. *At Any Cost: National Liberation Terrorism.*
Minneapolis: Lerner Publications Company, 2004.
This book offers a detailed look at nationalist terrorist groups, including the Kurdistan Workers Party (PKK). The book covers the history, formation, actions, and philosophies of such groups.

Kemal, Yasar. *Memed, My Hawk.* **New York: HarperCollins, 1993.**
Set in the mountains of Anatolia, this is the story of Memed, a young man who becomes a bandit because of a feudal landlord's injustice. The author is a pioneer in modern Turkish literature.

LoBaido, Anthony C., Yumi Ng, and Paul A. Rozario. *The Kurds of Asia.* **Minneapolis: Lerner Publications Company, 2003.**
Read about the Kurds of Turkey, Iran, and Iraq. They are the world's largest national group without a nation state.

Miller, Louise R. *Turkey: Between East and West.* **Tarrytown, NY: Benchmark Books, 1998.**
This book about Turkey is part of the Exploring Cultures of the World series for younger readers.

Orr, Tamra. *Turkey.* **New York: Children's Press, 2003.**
This book about Turkey is from the Enchantment of the World series for younger readers.

Settle, Mary Lee. *Turkish Reflections: A Biography of a Place.* **New York: Prentice Hall, 1991.**
Settle is an author who usually writes novels, including *Blood Tie*, which is set in Turkey. This is a travelogue that describes her travels through Turkey in 1989. Historical details of each place blend with personal observations.

Tekin, Latife. *Berji Kristin: Tales from the Garbage Hills: A Novel.* **Translated by Ruth Christie and Saliha Paker. London: Marion Boyars, 1993.**
Tekin tells a dark fairy tale about impoverished people in the 1960s who build huts on the site of a dump. The community on the outskirts of Istanbul struggles for survival and dignity and becomes known as Flower Hill.

Turkish Embassy.
<http://www.turkishembassy.org>
The embassy's site is a good place to start exploring Turkey. It provides information on Turkish art and culture, government and politics, business and economics, and more, as well as useful links to sites such as the English-language *Daily Turkish News*.

vgsbooks.com
<http://www.vgsbooks.com>
Visit vgsbooks.com, the homepage of the Visual Geography Series®, which is updated regularly. You can get linked to all sorts of useful on-line information, including geographical, historical, demographic, cultural, and economic websites.

Xenophon. *Anabasis: The March Up Country.* **Translated by W. H. D. Rouse. New York: New American Library, 1959.**
Xenophon gives a firsthand account of ten thousand Greek warriors making their way back from a disastrous military campaign in Persia through Asia Minor. Written in 401 B.C., this adventure story remains exciting reading.

Captions for photos appearing on cover and chapter openers:

Cover: The Hagia Sophia (from the Greek, meaning "Divine Wisdom") was originally a Christian basilica (large church) completed in A.D. 537. On May 29, 1453, Sultan Mehmet the Conqueror ordered it converted to a mosque (Islamic house of worship). It became a museum in the early twentieth century.

pp. 4–5 Some Christian art, such as the image of the Virgin Mary and the young Jesus *(left),* has been preserved in the interior of the Hagia Sophia. Many Islamic elements, such as the Arabic calligraphy *(center),* which translates, "God the Almighty," have been added.

pp. 8–9 Lake Van is surrounded by wild red poppies and snowcapped mountains.

pp. 22–23 Ruins of the ancient city of Troy, the setting of the Trojan War, may still be seen in Anatolia. The Greek poet Homer made Troy famous in his epics the *Iliad* and the *Odyssey.*

pp. 38–39 Young friends gather in front of a family home in Kars in eastern Turkey.

pp. 46–47 Elaborate symmetrical patterns characterize most Turkish carpets.

pp. 58–59 A market stall overflows with fresh fruit in Bodrum in southwestern Turkey.

Photo Acknowledgments

The images in this book are used with the permission of: © Kari Cornell, pp. 4–5, 48, 52, 58–59, 61, 62; © Digital Cartographics, pp. 6, 11; © Michele Burgess, pp. 8–9, 13, 38–39, 41, 46–47, 64; © Reza; Webistan/CORBIS, p. 10; © Art Directors/T. Richardson, p. 14; © Nevada Wier, p. 15; © Art Directors/ H. Gariety, p. 17; © Betty Crowell, p. 18; © Art Directors/Dorothy Burrows, p. 19; © Art Directors/Paul Petterson, p. 22–23; Library of Congress (LC-USZ62-93859), p. 24; © Mimmo Jodice/CORBIS p. 26; © Art Directors/TRIP, p. 28, 43; © Hulton-Deutsch Collection/CORBIS, p. 33; © GYORI ANTOINE/ CORBIS SYGMA, p. 35; © Michael Wallrath/Action Press/ZUMA Press, p. 36; © Art Directors/Helene Rogers, pp. 49, 50; © Pelletier Micheline/CORBIS SYGMA, p. 51; © Art Directors/Kate Clow, p. 55; © Art Directors/A. Tovy, p. 63; www.banknotes.com, p. 68 (all).

Cover: © Art Directors/Bob Turner. Back cover photo: NASA.